Dissenting Lives

This collection brings together a series of essays that combine the public and private nature of dissent, stories of dissent that encapsulate the mood of an historical or cultural period, or of a society. Dissent is most memorable when it is public, explosive, dramatically enacted. Yet quiet dissent is no less effective as a methodical unstitching of social and political mores, rules and regulations. Success depends, perhaps, less on intensity than on determination, on patience as much as courage. Moreover, although many persistent dissenters often gain an iconic status, most live dissent in the fabric of their ordinary lives. Some combine both. Imprisoned at Robben Island for 27 years, his image and voice erased from the print media or airwaves, Nelson Mandela remained, even in jail, one of the most powerful agents of dissent in South African society until his release in 1990. Deep connections, deep commitment, profoundly personal convictions and courageous public dissent are some of the threads that bind together this diverse and exciting collection of essays. Alone, each essay explores dissent and consent in stimulating and distinct ways; together, they speak both of the effects of dissent and consent and of their affective energies and potential.

This book was originally published as a special issue of *Life Writing*.

Anne Collett is an associate professor in the English Literatures Program at the University of Wollongong, Australia. She has edited *Kunapipi: Journal of Postcolonial Writing and Culture* since 2000 and has written extensively on post-colonial poetry and women's writing and visual arts, including most recently, essays on Jamaican Canadian poet Olive Senior and Australian poet, Judith Wright.

Tony Simoes da Silva teaches Literature at the University of Wollongong, Australia. Recent publications include work on displacement and identity as conveyed through literary representations of refugees; on civil conflict and gender in the work of Nigerian novelist, Chimamanda Ngozi Adichie; and on Australian film and literature.

Life Writing
Academic Editor: Maureen Perkins, Macquarie University, Australia

Life Writing, founded in 2004 by Mary Besemeres and Maureen Perkins, is one of the leading journals in the field of biography and autobiography.

Its title indicates that it reaches beyond traditional interpretations of biography and autobiography as genres belonging solely in the study of literature. It welcomes work from any discipline that discusses the nature of the self and self-expression and how these interact with the process of recording a life. Life writing is about expanding the ways in which we understand how lives are represented.

The journal has a special, though not exclusive, interest in cross-cultural experience. It also has the unique and unusual policy of carrying both scholarly articles and critically informed personal narrative. It is published four times a year and its editorial board comprises leaders in the field of life writing practice.

Book titles from *Life Writing* include:

Trauma Texts
Edited by Gillian Whitlock and Kate Douglas

Poetry and Autobiography
Edited by Jo Gill and Melanie Waters

International Life Writing Memory and Identity in Global Context
Edited by Paul Longley Arthur

Dissenting Lives
Edited by Anne Collett and Tony Simoes da Silva

Dissenting Lives

Edited by
Anne Collett and Tony Simoes da Silva

Routledge
Taylor & Francis Group

LONDON AND NEW YORK

First published 2015
by Routledge

2 Park Square, Milton Park, Abingdon, Oxon OX14 4RN
711 Third Avenue, New York, NY 10017, USA

Routledge is an imprint of the Taylor & Francis Group, an informa business

First issued in paperback 2017

British Library Cataloguing in Publication Data
A catalogue record for this book is available from the British Library

ISBN 13: 978-1-138-81011-2 (hbk)
ISBN 13: 978-1-138-05724-1 (pbk)

Typeset in Trebuchet MS
by RefineCatch Limited, Bungay, Suffolk

Publisher's Note
The publisher accepts responsibility for any inconsistencies that may have
arisen during the conversion of this book from journal articles to book chapters,
namely the possible inclusion of journal terminology.

Disclaimer
Every effort has been made to contact copyright holders for their permission to
reprint material in this book. The publishers would be grateful to hear from any
copyright holder who is not here acknowledged and will undertake to rectify
any errors or omissions in future editions of this book.

Contents

Citation Information

The chapters in this book were originally published in *Life Writing*, volume 8, issue 4 (December 2011). When citing this material, please use the original page numbering for each article, as follows:

Chapter 1
Editorial: Dissenting Lives
Anne Collett and Tony Simoes da Silva
Life Writing, volume 8, issue 4 (December 2011) pp. 351–359

Chapter 2
Consenting Voices? Activist Life Stories and Complex Dissent
Margaretta Jolly
Life Writing, volume 8, issue 4 (December 2011) pp. 363–374

Chapter 3
Detention, Displacement and Dissent in Recent Australian Life Writing
Michael Jacklin
Life Writing, volume 8, issue 4 (December 2011) pp. 375–385

Chapter 4
'The Closet of the Third Person': Susan Sontag, Sexual Dissidence, and Celebrity
Guy Davidson
Life Writing, volume 8, issue 4 (December 2011) pp. 387–397

Chapter 5
How to Avoid Life Writing: Lessons from David Lynch
Nicola Evans
Life Writing, volume 8, issue 4 (December 2011) pp. 399–409

Chapter 6
The Other Side of the Curtain
Irene Lucchitti
Life Writing, volume 8, issue 4 (December 2011) pp. 411–420

Chapter 7
Recomposing Her History: the Memoirs and Diaries of Ethel Smyth
Amanda Harris
Life Writing, volume 8, issue 4 (December 2011) pp. 421–431

Chapter 8
The Laws of God and Men: Eliza Davies' Story of an Earnest Life
Sarah Ailwood
Life Writing, volume 8, issue 4 (December 2011) pp. 433–444

Chapter 9
She Speaks with the Serpent's Forked Tongue: Expulsion, Departure, Exile and Return
Luz Hincapié
Life Writing, volume 8, issue 4 (December 2011) pp. 447–455

Please direct any queries you may have about the citations to
clsuk.permissions@cengage.com

Notes on Contributors

Sarah Ailwood is a lecturer in the Faculty of Law at the University of Canberra, Australia. Her research focuses on women's writing. Her current project investigates intersections between women's life writing, legal experience, law reform and ethics. Her other research interests include Jane Austen and Romantic women writers, men in women's texts, Katherine Mansfield and modernism. Sarah is also legally qualified and has worked in various legal professional roles. She currently convenes the first-year law programme at the UC.

Anne Collett is an associate professor in the English Literatures Program at the University of Wollongong, Australia. She publishes primarily on postcolonial poetry and women's writing, most recently including essays on Olive Senior, Judith Wright, Kamau Brathwaite and Emily Carr, and has edited a book on *The Unsociable Sociability of Women's Lifewriting* with Louise D'Arcens (Palgrave Macmillan, 2010). Anne is the editor of *Kunapipi: Journal of Postcolonial Writing and Culture*.

Guy Davidson teaches in the English Literatures Program, University of Wollongong, Australia. His research for the most part focuses on the inter-relations between sexuality, commodity culture and literary form in two main contexts: twentieth and twenty-first century US literature, and British and American literature of the late nineteenth and early twentieth centuries. He has published widely in journals such as *GLQ, Henry James Review, English Literature in Transition, Journal of Modern Literature* and *Australian Literary Studies*.

Nicola Evans holds degrees in English Literature from the University of Oxford, UK and a PhD in Communication Research from The Annenberg School, USA and now lectures in Media and Cultural Studies at the University of Wollongong, Australia. She is currently exploring the idea of 'backstage' in film and literature.

Amanda Harris completed her PhD at the University of New South Wales, Australia in 2009 with a thesis on 'Female Composers and Feminist Movements in England, France and Germany at the Turn of the Twentieth Century.' Recent articles explore the perspectives of early first-wave feminist movements on women in music and discuss what Ethel Smyth's unpublished correspondence reveals about her sexuality and romantic life. Amanda is currently broadening her interest in life writing by examining 1940s Australian diaries as a research associate at the University of Sydney, Australia and she lectures in the Musicology Program at the University of New South Wales, Australia.

Luz Hincapié received her MA in Postcolonial Literatures from the University of Wollongong, Australia (2002) and, after a year of teaching in Xi'an Technological University, China, returned to Bogotá where she worked at various universities and research institutes. Her publications and conferences centre on the topics of travel writing, migration and identity, Chicana/Latina literature in the USA, Asian diasporic literatures within Latin America and gender and postcolonial studies. Currently, she holds a University of Sydney International Scholarship in the Department of Gender and Cultural Studies. Her PhD research focuses on issues of race, identity and gender in the Japanese migration to Colombia.

Michael Jacklin is a research fellow in the School of English Literatures and Philosophy at the University of Wollongong, Australia where he is project officer on the multicultural subset of the AustLit database. His research interests include writing across cultures, exilic and diasporic writing, life writing and collaboration, Indigenous literatures and multicultural literature. His most recent publications focus on multilingual literatures in Australia and have appeared in *JASAL, Antipodes* and *Kunapipi*.

Margaretta Jolly co-directs the Centre for Life and Life Writing History Research at the University of Sussex, UK, and is reader in Education. She is editor of *Dear Laughing Motorbyke: Letters from Women Welders of the Second World War* (Scarlet, 1997) and *The Encyclopedia of Life Writing* (Routledge, 2001) and author of *In Love and Struggle: Letters and Contemporary Feminism* (Columbia University Press, 2008; winner of the Feminist and Women's Studies Association UK Book Prize, 2009).

Irene Lucchitti is a specialist in early twentieth-century Irish literature and culture, with expertise in life writing and translation studies. She studied the Irish language at the University of Sydney, Australia and completed her PhD in the English Language Program at the University of Wollongong, Australia where she is now an honorary fellow. She has published numerous articles and a book on the autobiography of Tomás O'Crohan of the Blasket Islands and is currently writing on a second Blasket writer, Peig Sayers. She is also following her work on the life writing of US performer Marta Becket with a study of the various writings and performances of singer-songwriter-novelist-lifewriter Jimmy Buffett.

Tony Simoes da Silva teaches in the English Literatures Program at the University of Wollongong, Australia. Recent or forthcoming publications include work on the figure of the refugee in contemporary world writing, as well as on African fiction and life writing. He is the author of *The Luxury of Nationalist Despair* (Rodopi, 2000) and co-editor of the journals *JASAL* and *La Questione Meridionale*.

Introduction
Dissenting Lives

During my lifetime I have dedicated myself to this struggle of the African people. I have fought against white domination, and I have fought against black domination. I have cherished the ideal of a democratic and free society in which all persons live together in harmony and with equal opportunities. It is an ideal which I hope to live for and to achieve. But if needs be, it is an ideal for which I am prepared to die. (Mandela, 'I Am the First Accused', p.133)

Dissent is most memorable when it is public, explosive, dramatically enacted. Yet quiet dissent is no less effective as a methodical unstitching of social and political mores, rules and regulations. Success depends, perhaps, less on intensity than on determination, and while Margaretta Jolly makes no such distinction when she refers to 'persistent dissenters' in her contribution to this collection, much of the writing she examines falls into the latter category. Moreover, although many persistent dissenters often gain an iconic status, most live dissent in the fabric of their ordinary lives. Some combine both, however unwittingly they may do so. Imprisoned at Robben Island for 27 years, his image and voice erased from the print media or airwaves, Nelson Mandela nevertheless remained even in jail one of the most powerful agents of dissent in South African society until his freedom in 1990. This quiet but persistent dissent against the apartheid regime emerged in the post-apartheid period as one of the most effective 'consenting dissenting voice[s]', to borrow again from Jolly's essay. Mandela's life story resonates strongly with the concerns of this special issue of *Life Writing*: from Jolly's opening essay the issue registers a dynamic understanding of the meaning of 'dissent', one that frequently evolves into consent and back again. Indeed, both her essay and Mandela's life story bring into focus another thread that emerges in the issue, one explored in a number of the contributions here collected—the role of the public intellectual as a dissenting voice but then also as a catalyst for new forms of consent. In the words of another iconic dissenter, Edward Said, writing in *Representations of the Intellectual* (1994):

> the public realm in which intellectuals make their representations is extremely complex, and contains uncomfortable features, but the meaning of an effective intervention in that realm has to rest on the intellectual's unbudgeable conviction in a concept of justice and fairness that allows for differences . . . (69)

That is no less the case of the anonymous dissenter, and one aspect highlighted in many of the essays is the role of the dissenter as an agent of change, alone or in a group. As we write, political and social scientists seek to make sense of one of the most dramatic moments of lived dissent on the global stage, the so-called Arab Spring revolution, with the influential magazine, *Foreign Affairs*, devoting much of its May/June 2011 issue to the topic. On one level a spectacular performance of dissent, the protests of millions of anonymous people across Tunisia, Algeria, Egypt and Syria have shown how individual voices came together to trigger change that is reverberating across vast and complex social structures.

Dissenting Lives brings together a series of essays that combine the public and private nature of dissent symbolised by the above examples. Each writer is concerned with stories of dissent that encapsulate the mood of an historical or cultural period, or of a society. *Dissenting Lives* came out of a symposium held at the University of Wollongong in 2010, organised by Anne Collett and Tony Simoes da Silva. Initially intended to bring together a series of discussion papers concerned with life writing and postcolonial themes and contexts, the event soon took off in a different direction. The title of the issue has evolved from an earlier iteration as 'Dissenting Voices', under which rubric these essays were presented at the workshop, and while a postcolonial framework might still apply to reading the texts discussed, most authors have avoided it. The shift recognises the direction the seminar itself took but also aptly reflects the substantial rewriting undertaken by most authors whose work is included in the issue. Margaretta Jolly herself responded to the papers presented at the workshop by revising her own argument, stressing in this final version the deeply intertwined nature of personal and collective dissent.

In 'Consenting Voices? Activist Life Stories and Complex Dissent', Jolly (this issue) explores the shifts that occur in the lives of 'persistent dissenters' as social and personal conditions change, but also as these dissenters age. The discussion considers whether 'life stories help us to understand patterns of dissent and consent' and 'turn[s] to some activist life writings and life stories to show that "dissent" is often likely to become "consent", but not necessarily with any less political commitment and effect.' Quoting words by Carole Hanisch in her essay, 'The Personal is Political', Jolly considers how dissent is performed, produced and consumed in a complex traffic where the act of dissent so often is co-opted into a broader discourse of 'manufactured consent', to cite Noam Chomsky's memorable phrase. After a brief overview of main trends in '[s]ocial movement theory', Jolly notes, in words especially apt to this issue, that '[t]he birth of a social movement needs an initiating event that will begin a chain reaction of events' and that '[t]ypically activist leaders lay the ground with interventions designed to spark a movement.' Setting out a framework for a wide-ranging discussion of life writing by political and social activists, she writes:

> Social movement theory helps us see dissidents' life writings as part of historical patterns as well as processes. It also helps us to explain how the same person can be both dissenting and consenting, insider and outsider, as they live through the life cycle of a movement.

Coincidentally, in June 2011, as the collection was being assembled, Noam Chomsky was awarded the Sydney Peace Prize by the Sydney Peace Foundation. One of the world's best known dissenters, Chomsky has lived his life on a stage from where he has performed his dissent persistently and courageously. Very often a lone voice raging against the system, he has also played a crucial role as a Pied Piper leading dissenting masses calling for change and for freedom. Famously the co-author of *Manufacturing Consent* (with Edward Herman), Chomsky has dedicated his life to unstitching the more or less visible ways in which dissent is policed, discouraged, denied. As a public intellectual, Chomsky has made the most of an ability to think aloud, to prevaricate in verbal and written performance. Like Mandela, Chomsky symbolises a commitment to the power of the dissenting voice that provides an apt background to this issue.

Indeed, Chomsky was awarded his prize soon after the whirlwind of dissent made its way round the Middle East, its actors drawing, however unconsciously, on the beliefs Chomsky made synonymous with his life; and there too a single agent of change is said to have triggered the revolution of the masses. Unlike Chomsky, however, Mohamed Bouazizi performed his dissent not in the powerful language of intellectual and academic discourse but in the only way be believed he had at his disposal: by setting himself alight in public. Bouazizi's dissent served as a catalyst for a series of acts that have now seen the collapse of a number of dictatorships in the Middle East and the intensification of civil rebellions. In 'Terrorism After the Revolutions: How Secular Uprisings Could Help (or Hurt) Jihadists', one of the many expert opinion pieces published since Bouazizi's death, Daniel Byman links Bouazizi's spectacular but paradoxically rather private dissent to the toppling of dictators in Tunisia and Egypt and even to what he perceives as a decrease in Al Qaeda's influence. The essays in this collection all have something in common with these political and intellectual threads.

In 'Detention, Displacement and Dissent in Recent Australian Life Writing', for example, Michael Jacklin (this issue) explores one of the most fraught issues in Australian society—that of reception accorded refugees and asylum seekers. At one end of the spectrum are those who believe Australia is failing its ethical and legal obligations in its treatment of such individuals; at the other end are those Australians who insist that the country has an inalienable right to select whom it admits as would-be Australians. Caught in the middle of these heated dissenting conflicts are the refugees and asylum seekers themselves who have exercised their own forms of embodied dissent by sewing their lips in a vow of silence and starvation (Mares; MacCallum). In his essay, Jacklin takes up the persistence of the dissenting voice on the contentious issue of refugees and asylum seekers in contemporary Australia. Noting that '[r]efugee issues have been a factor in every Australian election over the past ten years', Jacklin sets out to consider the role of refugee narratives in these fractious debates. Specifically, he is concerned with 'whether refugee narratives have a wider effect on the public debate in Australia regarding refugees and detention'. In a discussion of two such life writing narratives, Mahboba Rawi's *Mahboba's Promise* (2005) and Najaf Mazari's *The Rugmaker of Mazar-e-Sharif* (2008), Jacklin ponders the subtleties of dissent in different settings, national and political, and the internal tensions of works caught up in the conflicting currents of protest, of assimilation and rejection, where the refugee negotiates complex nationalist ideologies of home and exile, of belonging and alienation. Writing with Mazari's text in mind, Jacklin states that '[n]ot all refugee narratives are propelled by acts of dissent' and that 'Mazari has opted to avoid dissent wherever possible.' Indeed, he proposes that '*The Rugmaker of Mazar-e-Sharif* is the story of a refugee learning to cope and adapt, with dissent playing little part in this narrative of a dislocated life.'

In a move that further complicates the collection's focus on the narrative of dissent, Nicola Evans (this issue) asks at the outset of her discussion: 'Must our stories be told at all?', and goes on to remark:

> [that her] goal here is not to undermine the value of life writing, but to suggest that the genres of life writing might be usefully extended to include forms of anti-life writing, strategies of "life withholding" emerging in the wake of the boom in forms of confessional narrative proliferating across media.

In a detailed discussion of filmmaker David Lynch, Evans draws on film auteur theory to examine Lynch's calculated subversion of the celebrity status of the auteur. Evans situates Lynch's work and his persona as auteur within a broader discourse in which the life of the work of art is inseparable from that of its creator. In the Jamesonian postmodern movement, authorship is framed and authenticated by marketing and advertising campaigns in which the author is expected to participate. Evans asserts:

> A host of extratextual materials accompany the release of films and books like an expanding entourage clustering around a star. Driven by the multiplication of distribution channels and the hunger for more and more content, both books and films come with a generous collection of promotional and behind the scenes information.

Co-opted by the publicity campaigns for his films as a mouthpiece for creative genius, the auteur, Lynch, finds refuge in a playful banality that offers up the superficial self of consumer society. At the heart of Evans' essay is a fascination with the ways in which Lynch simultaneously engages the paratext (Genette) designed to supplement his work and to deflate and deflect its power and function. For Evans, 'Lynch is a master of deflecting the gaze of the consumer elsewhere' and it is this ambivalence that 'makes the satellite texts doubly interesting'. Yet, despite what she identifies as Lynch's mastery at side-stepping consumerist discourses where the work of art exists only insofar as the author is willing to collaborate in hawking it, Evans remarks on the 'the sheer volume of talk that David Lynch has put on record', much of it *about* him.

In '"The Closet of the Third Person": Susan Sontag, Sexual Dissidence, and Celebrity', Guy Davidson (this issue) focuses on selected writings by Susan Sontag to examine the private/public divide in the life writing of celebrity literati. On one level, an intellectual who came to be known for her iconoclastic thinking, Sontag restrained her dissent to a public arena in which her personal life was a no-go area. Drawing on Jonathan Dollimore's work on sexual dissidence, Davidson notes that his 'aim is neither to upbraid Sontag for her lack of openness, nor to express disappointment that such an influential individual should have proved unwilling to come out and more definitively'. Davidson proceeds to tease out in her writing some of the 'ways in despite or indeed because of her reticence, queer sexuality centrally informed her career'. Focusing in his essay on a juxtaposition of Sontag's canonical *Against Interpretation* and 'a recently published selection from Sontag's journals and notebooks', *Reborn*, Davidson sets out to answer the question:

> [i]f in her essays Sontag implicitly and self-reflexively raises the possibility of an autobiographical reading of a prose famous for its impersonality, what difference does it make that we now have available the journals in which the first person, rather than being covertly expressed, dramatically emerges?

The essay's concern with the persistent tension between private and public and with the ways in which dissent perhaps can only ever be public resonates strongly with Jolly's work. Sontag's refusal to allow readers to see her private self in her essays, despite the obvious traces, suggests how the dissenting voice inevitably presupposes a dissenting life. In a point that is echoed in some of the other essays in the collection, Davidson suggests that the act of speaking out against something necessitates a personal, embodied commitment if it is to be read or seen as authentic and credible. In a sense, to dissent is to out oneself as more or less ready and willing to be co-opted into public discourses of protest and transformation, in this instance sexual. As he remarks:

> For Sontag, queer sexuality lies at the heart of contradictory desires to expose oneself and to hide within writing. These contradictory desires were to be played out in a career as a celebrity writer who barred talk of her queerness, and in an impersonal writing which encoded the deeply personal fact of queerness.

Echoing Jolly's paper, Davidson too offers an interesting twist on the view 'that "dissent" is often likely to become "consent"'.

The same could also be said of the 'lives' of Ethel Smyth, a relatively unknown/unheard composer (relative that is to her male peers) whose memoirs gave her the public face, the public acclaim, and as deafness increased, the public voice her music did not. The act of writing against the grain—writing that put the case for a politics of gender that repeatedly marginalised her music—became a force for inclusion, not necessarily in the musical canon, but in a literary canon. Although Amanda Harris claims that 'it is possible to see [Smyth's] writing as an opportunity that she came to regard not as merely complementary to her music but as essential to its survival into posterity', Harris' essay reveals the degree to which Smyth's memoirs, and increasingly, her diaries, gave her power over the construction and reception of her (creative) life that was otherwise unavailable to her:

> The memoirs, intended as an authoritative source that would convince the public of Smyth's value as a composer, were designed to have an impact on the current reality of her life. The diaries, containing more nuanced reflections...were designed as a historical record which might outlast her and provide an authoritative account of her life for future researchers.

In light of this, we might understand this 'life' as guided and energised by (feminist) dissent, and yet, although this is certainly true, we might also understand the alternative form of creative output as a form of consent. A 'significant change in [Smyth's] outlook on life following her loss of hearing, which coincided with the publication of her first book, is indicative of how central writing was to the recovery of her creative persona', observes Harris, but in allowing her 'to continue beyond the loss of her ability to appreciate music', writing, and in particular, life writing, gave Smyth an eager public to whom she consented whilst in the very act of dissent. Although Smyth acknowledges the significant role her writing played in the performance of her musical works, she also notes that it was for her writing that she had 'become quite famous', and it was to this public that she played in the latter part of her life.

To whom did Eliza Davies play? In *The Story of an Earnest Life: A Woman's Adventures in Australia, and Two Voyages Around the World*, published in 1881, Davies claims that she wrote out of duty and published her life of 'trials, temptations, pain, privation, persecution, and exposure' that others might derive strength and hope from her victory over adversity and the success of her dissent. This dissent not only took the form of a classic feminist dissent from 'nineteenth-century imperial ideologies of marriage and domesticity', but in what Sarah Ailwood (this issue) describes as 'the absence of state-sanctioned legal guidance or redress', Davies dissents from the unsympathetic avenue of colonial law to free her from a violently abusive husband, and turns, in part, to biblical argument for aid. Interestingly, the means she finds to address her problems and to effectively construct a form of dissent that will serve her ends, presents its own difficulties. As Ailwood observes, 'For Davies, the New Testament tradition failed not only in its limited models of empowered female selfhood, but also in its models of victimised female selfhood': Davies records how, on the night of her final flight from her husband, she realised that Jesus 'could not sympathize with me, because he was not a woman...He was never situated as I then was.' But the 'missionary memoir', popularised by female missionaries during the 1830s and 1840s, provided Davies with a genre that 'offered women whose experience did not reflect the culturally-approved roles of wife and mother a model for reflectively interpreting their lives that was sanctioned by alternative religious ideologies'. The 'life' that Davies chooses and constructs for her public is to a large degree self-fashioned, but it is also one that draws on the strengths and reveals the weakness of the various competing or complementary discourses available. In this case, 'alternative modes of life writing enable Davies to construct a self that is independent of her husband, in text if not in law.' It is in this text that Davies describes the herculean task of investigating and preparing evidence to prove the case for divorce, and the harrowing act of writing her deposition: '... while writing of cruel deeds, I seemed to be living in the dark past, with all my dead hopes scattered around me. Tongue cannot tell what torture I suffered while writing that document.' But her tongue is enabled by the memoir, and although it is a tale of much suffering—suffering consequent in part upon Davies' dissent from husband, society and the law, it is a suffering that will be relieved in ultimate success—a success that she tellingly attributes not to the law of men, but to the law of God to whom she has consented: 'When the decision of the Court was written on parchment, how did I feel? My prayer had been heard and answered by a prayer-hearing and prayer-answering God, and I was legally and morally free.' The 'life' makes clear a self-hood achieved in large part through writing—on Court parchment, in the New Testament of the disciples and the memoirs of female missionaries, in Davies' legal deposition and ultimately, in her autobiography.

The life of Marta Becket affords the reader no such release. Hers is the most profound and the most desultory of dissenting lives. In Irene Lucchitti's essay (this issue), 'The Other Side of the Curtain', she reveals how a performed life took such an extreme form of dissent as to subsume that life in a fantasy of life. Self and other participate in a ghostly performance of present absence. Becket performed a solo-life on the stage of an abandoned theatre in Death Valley Junction to, as often as not, an empty house—empty that is, except for the Renaissance audience she painted on the walls of her self-styled Amargosa Opera House. Her act, initially hosted by her husband, was performed after his death as if he had been there—offering a theatrical rendition of his absence by leaving gaps in the spaces he would have filled and painting him into the backdrop. Lucchitti remarks on 'the psychological slippage' that is revealed in Becket's described negotiation of the passage between the life of imagination and the life of the 'real' world: 'As she emerges from the experience, life seems wooden while Art is a living thing.' Hers is a deeply unsettling and poignant story of dissent from 'the world'—she is 'her own closed circuit'. Yet, 'while [Becket] states repeatedly throughout the text that her central relationship is with her self and her imagination and that she is her own best friend, it is clear,' writes Lucchitti, 'that her self continues to elude her in this written performance of a staged life.' 'Life is a stage,' writes Becket, in a performance of words many times performed, to which she adds her own reflection—a reflection that disappears into a hall of mirrors: 'Millions of plays are going on at once. I didn't realise that I, too, was a part of this drama. I was too busy observing and recording it.' Somehow in the observing and recording, it would seem that Becket lost sight of which side of the curtain she was on—the curtain that acts as a line between the real and the performed, player and character, actor and audience, turns out to be something of a smoke screen in which 'Marta Beckett' is more 'lost' than found.

This is the territory of the threshold that is so difficult and dangerous to negotiate: 'Writing is the most daring thing I have ever done and the most dangerous,' declares Gloria Anzaldúa. 'Writing is dangerous because we are afraid of what the writing reveals . . . Yet in that very act lies our survival because a woman who writes has power.' Life writing is situated in the dangerous borderlands, a place where the writer is vulnerable, but it is here that Luz Hincapié believes academic writing should also be situated. Her essay explores her own life in relation to the lives she hopes to write about. It is an act in part of self-ethnography and an act that requires a giving of self to other. Drawing on the work of Ruth Behar, Hincapié explores the uses of 'a writing that is vulnerable; a self-ethnographical writing which takes us somewhere we couldn't otherwise go and moves us beyond inertia to identify intensely with those one is writing about.' The essay takes the opportunity not only to explore a dissenting form of academic writing, but to acknowledge the dissenting voices of foremothers like Behar and Anzaldúa who 'forged new ways of writing about Self and Other which are far from a dispassionate and distant authoritative voice.' Here Hincapié also explores the borderlands between past and present, child self and adult self, home of birth and home of adoption. Hers is the story of the immigrant, and it is the story of the lives of immigrants she wishes to write; but in order not to get lost, in her own life and in the lives of others, both of which threaten to overwhelm her, she must find a means of negotiating the territory between self and other. Making her path between distance and intimacy, between dissent and consent, Hincapié writes of the struggle to become a cultural translator and to tell a story of the lives of others with integrity: 'I want to be able to speak—with my forked tongue—about my experience with more detachment and about my research participants with all the fire of feeling in the hope of drawing deep connections.' Deep connections, deep commitment, profoundly personal convictions and courageous public dissent are some of the threads that bind together this diverse and exciting collection of essays. Alone, each essay explores dissent and consent in stimulating and distinct ways; together, they speak both of the effects of dissent and consent and of their affective energies and potential.

References

Byman, Daniel. 'Terrorism After the Revolutions: How Secular Uprisings Could Help (or Hurt) Jihadists.' *Foreign Affairs* May/June 2011: 48–54.

Chomsky, Noam, and Edward S. Herman. *Manufacturing Consent: The Political Economy of the Mass Media*. London: Vintage, 1994.

Genette, Gérard. *Paratexts. Thresholds of Interpretation*. Trans. Jane E. Lewin Cambridge: Cambridge University Press, 1997.

Huxley, John. 'Sydney Peace Prize Goes to Chomsky.' *The Age* [Australia] 2 June 2011. Web. 30 July 2011. http://www.theage.com.au/national/sydney-peace-prize-goes-to-chomsky-20110601-1fgws.html

MacCullum, Mungo. *Girt by Sea: Australia, the Refugees and the Politics of Fear.* Melbourne, Victoria: Black Ink, 2002.

Mandela, Nelson. 'I Am the First Accused.' Pretoria, 20 April 1964. *Speeches that Changed the World.* London: Murdoch Books, 2008: 130–33.

Mares, Peter. *Borderline: Australia's Response to Refugees and Asylum Seekers in the Wake of the Tampa.* Sydney: U. of NSW Press, 2002.

Said, Edward. *Representations of the Intellectual.* London: Virago, 1994.

Anne Collett and Tony Simoes da Silva

Consenting Voices? Activist Life Stories and Complex Dissent

Margaretta Jolly

What can life stories reveal about political dissenters who were once on the margins but have moved centrewards? This journey is one that many activist autobiographers have taken, from the academic Karla Jay (formerly in the lesbian rights group Lavender Menace) to the spectacular example of President Obama after writing his memoir *Dreams From My Father*. Do life stories help us to understand patterns of dissent and consent? Can they indeed balance judgements about insiders, outsiders and traitors to the cause? I will argue that they can, particularly when illuminated by theories of social movement cycles and the life course. I will also reflect upon my own life story work with feminist 'veterans' to open a space for thinking about the subtle relation between consent and dissent, especially when we take the long view of activism by ageing and aged subjects.

Carole Hanisch was a founding member of New York Radical Women and originator of the Miss America Protest in 1968. In 1969, she authored the groundbreaking paper, 'The Personal is Political', a conviction still evident from her website today. In this light, consider this letter she wrote to a feminist friend in 1989:

> Life has been damn hard for most everyone I know—both in and out of "the Movement" [...] these past ten or so years. I have had some pretty bad bouts of depression and burnout, and even some times when I've had to focus on just getting through to keep from going down all the way. The worst was in the early '80s when the full impact of the 'sacrifices' began to hit home—turning 39 with no man in sight and with little hope of having a child and the introspection that comes with that. Even having a man in my life some of those years didn't help a whole lot.

A trip to Nicaragua in 1985 in support of the Sandinista Revolution was an enormous help as it focused my attention on something other than "self" and put my problems into a broader perspective. Noone completely escaped the "Me-ism" of the '80s; it wasn't just a Yuppie disease. I think it's in large part due to the isolation, self-imposed and forced on us by our culture (or lack of it).[...]

I know the panic and fear that getting older engenders—especially without money and family. But in my dread, I try to remember it's not, at root, a problem of, or for, my comrades individually, or even of the Movement, but of this stinking, decaying capitalist system. [...] I certainly haven't solved the immediate and future problems of relative poverty and time to do political work. What I miss most is the Movement with its forward thrust, community, sense of purpose, excitement of new discoveries and victories. I miss the Movement more than I miss a child, money or even a man. It's lacking all that's really the pits. And having a child or a man without the Movement to make things more equal is more work, more oppression, more exhaustion. (qtd. in Jolly, *In Love and Struggle* 243–4)

Few, I imagine, could be untouched by Hanisch's honesty about personal struggle in the midst of political battle. And it stokes my admiration for persistent dissenters, for people who just won't give up. But many people are not as persistent or as brave as Hanisch. And it is not uncommon now to find that movement veterans have woken up in middle or late age to find themselves consultants or lawyers, or academics indeed, with less time for activism, less appetite. What do we make of the fact that so many veterans of the big social movements of the 1960s find themselves now in positions of power, or at least of professional responsibility that have transformed earlier ideas of how to do dissidence? What does this mean in terms of the political impact of those movements and of the strategies of those individuals? And for society as a whole?

Of course these are questions about the nature of change and of history, as well as of psychology. This article has not the space to address the complex question of what counts as a movement's 'success', though this may include achieving legislation and policy change, changing public opinion and increasing equality (Della Porta and Diani 226–50).What I want to do instead is to nuance this special issue's theme of life writing as a form of dissenting voice and ask what it can tell us about the real and muddy contexts of activism and its choices. Do life stories help us to understand patterns of dissent and consent? Can they indeed undo judgements about insiders, outsiders and traitors to the cause? To do so, I will begin looking at sociologists who analyse the pattern of social movements as a whole. I will use this to reflect on the perspectives of some activist life writers who have arguably moved centrewards. I will then reflect on the effect of age on activism, arguing that life course theory can work alongside social movement theory to further explain how the same person can be a firebrand at one moment and a civil servant the next and sometimes simultaneously. Finally, I want to turn to some activist life writings and life stories to show that 'dissent' is often likely to become 'consent', but not necessarily with any less political commitment or effect.

Social Movement Theory and the Life Cycle of a Group

Social movement theory provides tools for understanding dissent as a social phenomenon that can be found in all societies but with specific features. Some approaches to theorising social movements, roughly in chronological order, have included Marxism, structural functionalism and relative deprivation theory, value-added theory, resource mobilisation frame analysis, social constructionist theory and new social movement theory. All these theories start from the point of view that social movements arise when social groups are polarised around conflict, with clearly identified opponents, and that they occur in both authoritarian and democratic societies. But they are differently pitched. The first theories focused on labour or nationalist protests, based on Marxist ideas of class conflict, though in the United States, theories of crowd behaviour took this in a more psychological direction (Davies; Gurr). A second wave of theory, which gained ground in the 1960s and 1970s, by contrast focuses on a movement's organisation, building on the work of Max Weber and the American sociological tradition. It suggests that dissent reflects not so much social upset but the ability to mobilise resources. Activists from this perspective are not angry or sorrowful people driven by ideology or social conflict. They are skilful organisers who discuss strategies and weigh up the costs and benefits as well as opportunities for action (Oberschall). Charles Tilly, a leading theorist of resource mobilisation, defines big social movements as a series of contentious performances, displays and campaigns by which ordinary people make collective claims on others.

A third form of analysis in turn finds resource mobilisation approaches to be ahistorical-too much about the how and not enough about the why. European post-Marxist sociologists such as Alain Touraine and Alberto Melucci, in particular, argued that social movements of the 1960s and 1970s were distinctively 'new' in style and demand. The women's movement, anti-racism/civil rights, gay rights, student movements, environmental movements and the peace movement, for example, presented more than mobilised resources (Touraine; Melucci, Keane and Mier). Neither were they primarily defined by Marxian models of class conflict. They emphasised group identity, lifestyles and personal change, and were characterised by radical mobilisation tactics: direct action, non violent civil disobedience and a diffuse network rather than hierarchical central organisation. They emerged from middle rather than working class constituencies. The general explanation is that these are 'post-materialist' movements, motivated by quality of life issues and enabled by economic security, expanded civil society and democratisation, even as they drew on a crisis of credibility in Western-style party democracy.

Social movement theory also observes a cyclical pattern to such movements, as they spark, grow, consolidate and then start to make decisions, for example, about maintaining themselves versus recruiting, about lobbying versus integrating (Tarrow). The birth of a social movement needs an initiating event that will begin a chain reaction of events, for example, Rosa Parks riding in the whites-only section of the bus in segregated North America (Smelser). Typically, activist leaders lay the ground with interventions designed to spark a movement. This initiating event is followed by a coalescing of the movement through specific campaigns that attempt to communicate to a broader audience. Della Porta and Diani explain that:

> the concepts of cycles, waves, or campaigns all attempt to describe and explain periods of intensified protest. As in cultures and the economies, there is indeed a recurrent dynamic of ebb and flow in collective mobilisation. In particular, by demonstrating the vulnerability of the authorities, the first movements to emerge lower the cost of collective action for other actors. In addition, the victories they obtain undermine the previous order of things, provoking counter-mobilisation. (189)

To accept that social movements have their own life cycle suggests that whether a movement succeeds or fails in its objective, it eventually dissolves in its original form. On one level, its core cannot survive institutionalisation, even though institutionalisation may be part of its objective.

Letters, Memoirs and the Age of a Movement

Social movement theory helps us see dissidents' life writings as part of historical patterns as well as processes. It also helps us to explain how the same person can be both dissenting and consenting, insider and outsider, as they live through the life cycle of a movement. At the same time, it may be that their various life writings betray ambivalence or regrets about a movement's trajectory. Let me give you an example from my research on letter writing in the Anglo-American women's liberation movement in the 1970s and 1980s. Initially, I was over-whelmed by the intense emotions of these letters, double-edged gifts and demands as often angry as they were loving. I was also fascinated by their intensely polemical features and what they showed about the movement's internal conventions and subcultures. But the letters were greatly illuminated when I saw they were part of a collective 'relationship history' governed by a dialectic of separation and integration ('Three Ways to End a Relationship: Letter Writing and the Dialectics of Political Separatism'). These were traces of a social movement that was in a phase of expansion but also of internal struggle as it gained power and clarity. They were historically part of the phase of feminism that lived first under the sign of sisterhood and then under what Rita Felski called 'the doxa of difference'—as the movement faced issues of formalisation—often more ambivalently than other movements less committed to personal change. The sense of loss that Hanisch expresses in her letter to a feminist friend expresses her alienation from this later phase.

Social movement theory also helps us to situate movement memoirs. As many have observed, these often take the form of secular rebirth narrative, written to confess of early ignorance and then to teach and preach. The classic here is Malcolm X's autobiography, pivoted upon his dual religious and political conversion to the Nation of Islam. These memoirs tend to be written in the early, expanding phase of a movement (X and Haley). But what happens to this satisfying structure in memoirs written after it has dispersed or bureaucratised? Here is a snippet from Karla Jay's 1999 *Tales of the Lavender Menace: A Memoir of Liberation*:

> It is hard for me to explain how the protagonist of this memoir emerged as a tenured full professor and director of women's studies. It took me sixteen years to complete my degree. After all those years I thought New York University would present me with a retirement present rather than a doctorate. I toiled for many years as an adjunct professor, and now I've been at Pace University in New York City for a quarter of a century. A preppie academic in Brooks Brothers blazers, blouses, and flannel pants, I bear little resemblance to my younger incarnation. Instead of plotting the peaceful overthrow of the system, I sit through endless committee meetings where some colleagues visibly cringe at words like "precedent" and "change". My evenings are spent hunched over unmarked term papers and drafts of scholarly essays. In my spare time I scan the Internet for stocks that will speed my way to a capitalistic retirement in a gentler climate. Nowadays a night of debauchery is likely to entail a trip to a gourmet emporium to fondle the grapes and sample the extra virgin olive oil. [...] As I revisited the exploits of the lesbian/feminist radical with the unkempt hair and utopian ideals, I often felt I was writing about someone else, some long-dead, distant relative whose name escapes me. (263)

This sense of bemused nostalgia is quite typical of a relatively large group of memoirs recently published by radicals who came of age in the 1960s and 1970s: others include Sheila Rowbotham, Yasmin Alibhai-Brown, Tariq Ali, Jane Gallop and Joan Coxsedge. The conversion narrative has had to be modified in a way that Malcolm X never lived to write. Jay tells her early political coming of age in a riot of sex, sun and protest. But the excerpt above comes from an epilogue, leaving a long gap of the years in which 'dissent', at the institutional level, becomes 'consent'. This part of the activist's story often forms a different kind of confession, not of former ignorance later to be transformed but of a guiltily comfortable survival. Margaret Henderson's study of Australian feminists' memoirs concludes that 'for a movement that did so much in a couple of decades, it is surprising how non-triumphal, uncelebratory or, at least, modest, the memories have been' (*Marking Feminist Times* 240).[1]

This guilt extends to writing the autobiography itself. Lynne Segal opens her 2007 *Making Trouble: Life and Politics* with the sentence 'This is not a memoir' (1). In a recent piece, 'Who Do You Think You Are? Feminist Memoir Writing', she explains why (1). First, she does not want to equate history with memory, sensitive as she is to the historical and ideological construction of both. Second, she is concerned about the context of self-disclosure—its individualism, its false promises of an authentic self and intimate experience, its navet about the market. Third, she is worried about the politics of autobiographical writing for socialist feminists in particular. She will have us know that feminist conscious-ness-raising is *not* the same as misery memoir!

Historians of the 'second wave' largely agree that the movement cannot be named as such any more. But they are divided on whether feminist activism in its current form is succeeding or not, and indeed, whether the earlier campaigns left an adequate political base on which to do so.[2] Segal is an optimist, but sees herself writing in a context of political gloom, of being a 'relic' of an age of faith. She ends by justifying her guilty autobiography-writing as an effort at creating political legacy, consenting to the politics of publishing as well as those of the state, university and media. Is one aspect of this internal negotiation due to the fact that she is writing long after the dissolution phase of her particular social movement? If we read writings from those coming to contemporary 'new' social movements such as transsexual or autistics liberation, or the global justice movement, we naturally find less talk of legacy and gloom. Indeed, we often find conversion narratives in which it is easier to imagine a pure form of dissenting voice (Prosser; Williams; Klein).

Life Course Theory, Generation and Dissent

Just as activists' life writings will be marked by their point on a movement's age, naturally they bear the stamp of their own ageing as well (Giugni). It would be foolish to disregard the degree to which Hanisch's letter to a friend reflects middle age and Jay's memoir, life in her 60s. In many ways, the waxing and waning of 'dissent' is defined by life stage. Yet it would be equally foolish to predict that all youthful dissidents will turn conservative as they age or follow some universalised 'seven ages of (wo)man'. In contrast, socio-demographic 'life course' studies analyse sequences of life as culturally specific.[3] The life stages of second wave feminists, for example, should be situated initially within the 'age cohort generation' of Baby Boomers (born 1946–1964), which grew up in the period of unprecedented prosperity and technological change that followed World War II. Many studies suggest that people of this generation in Western countries are generally individualistic free agents with high interest in self-fulfilment through personal growth. They have demonstrated 'a strong work ethic and high job involvement, which has led to economic security and career success, although often at the expense of their personal lives' (Egri and Ralston 9).

Elements of this description seem at odds with the collectivist ideals of second wave feminists, but it tells us as importantly about their more conventional peers and the conditions of affluence that defined new opportunities and questions for the white, middle class majority (Edmunds). Activists came of age when *relative* material comfort, expanded higher education, economic opportunities and welfare systems may have allowed introspection and a high degree of individual self-definition even as they also provoked anger at exclusion and contradictory opportunities. Historians of social movements tend to see the Baby Boom generation as highly idealistic, but admit that in many ways, they came of age during a time of general idealism (Giugni). They also admit that the children of the classic activist generation of the 1960s have been less able to afford their parents' confident rebellion, economically and psychologically. Lois Benjamin's analysis of the 'generational consciousness' of African Americans, for example, draws out the effects of desegregation in terms of a generation that 'adopted the individualistic value system of the dominant group [...] especially for those who were born or who came of age after the civil rights era' (ix).

Life course studies also point towards a socially nuanced understanding of life stages and 'critical life events', such as childbirth and divorce. Many memoirs are written as part of a process of life review, coming to terms with old age and the decline of physical, if not intellectual, power. Activists, unsurprisingly, reject conventional narratives that equate ageing with social disengagement, and, of course, a significant minority are already older when they join a movement. Life course theorists argue that political withdrawal may instead reflect post-industrial society's exclusion and abjection of older people (Bornat). Molly Andrews was provoked by this very idea to study the life histories of 15 British men and women aged between 70 and 90 who had remained active socialists, finding that it was activism itself that provided the key to their late life resilience.

Yet undoubtedly, life writings by older or elderly activists offer 'dissent' with a very different flavour. Segal rejects the confessional mode, but when she writes about the love of her life leaving her for a younger woman when she was in her 50s, her suffering is evident. Her earlier commitments to anti-sexist alliances with men give way to newly radical thoughts on older women's sexual rights. Similarly, Michele Roberts ends her memoir *Paper Houses* with a painfully honest weighing up of losses and gains in her search for a 'home' in the counterculture. Age retains a powerful hold over the life story, for some, defining further political challenges over the conditions of ageing, for others, offering a buffer of private life around the public. We need then to analyse the relationship between the writer's age at the time of writing and the age that they are writing about. This is by no means always one of conservative looking back at radical youth, but a more complex process of life review and internal as well as external settlement.

We can see how difficult it is to assess the politics of such exercises in life review, to disentangle what is the effect of their place in the life cycle of the movement, what results from the individual's age at the time of writing and what reflects their generational cohort, as well as the effect of the general historical period in question—particularly as that itself constructs specific age identities. Older radicals' representation of their teenage years is particularly interesting in this light. Patricia Spacks argues that twentieth century autobiographies are generally characterised by a fascination with adolescence, a fascination I would argue that endures in twenty-first century life writings. Adolescence occurs in all societies, but on another level, is 'invented' when industrialisation allows it to materialise as a longish phase of life. We can test this by looking at eighteenth century autobiographies, which hurry over the teenage years to get to the adult in their prime, and nineteenth century ones, which instead dwell endlessly on childhood. Spacks considers that the greater individualism of twentieth century life, by contrast, allowed a new valuing of the years of rebellion:

> Adolescence, Erikson has explained, finding words for a general feeling which certainly pre-dated his pronouncement [...] is a time of moratorium, a space *between*. Its peculiar freedom allows the young person to oppose the status quo often with relatively little penalty. (206)

On one level, therefore, Spacks' vision shows *all* late modern life writers think themselves to be dissenting voices, 'young men and women who, unlike ourselves, have not yet given hostages to fortune, do not need to conform' (207). But she also helps us to see why activists might particularly dwell on their adolescent or youthful years. Commenting on autobiographies by Ann Moody, Malcolm X and Maxine Hong Kingston, Spacks concludes that:

> The autobiographical records of members of minority groups, for whom the likelihood of affecting society often disappears in the hard struggles of everyday survival, emphasize this point by their own use of the material of adolescence. (211)

In a similar vein, we could understand the years of early second wave feminism (and particularly lesbian feminism) as powerfully coinciding with the exploration of independence and love that takes place in one's 20s, the age of the majority in the movement, who were also precisely the age of the later 'Baby Boom cohort'. Erik Erikson defines this stage of life as a struggle of 'intimacy versus isolation', and I would argue that we can see this in letters between women of the period, even as feminists were challenging masculinised ideals of autonomy (qtd. in Spacks, 101). By contrast, feminist activists' mid-years in the 1980s and 1990s unfolded during a context of Cold War tensions, privatising economies and neo-colonial settlements (Whitbourne and Willis). In Eriksonian terms, the 30s and 40s are years of 'generativity versus stagnation' (103), in which accomplishments and failures begin to be measured. Again, Hanisch's letter speaks to this moment. Though she challenges reproduction as a woman's *raison d'tre*, she remains afraid that she has generated neither political nor biological 'children' (qtd. in Jolly, *In Love and Struggle*, pp.243–244).

Barack Obama's autobiography is an intriguing test case for a life course analysis in this respect. Unusually, composed in mid-life at a moment of professional success, it was written on the back of an advance given him as the first African-American president of the *Harvard Law Review* when he was just 33. A straightforward story of growing up and finding his identity, and a familiar father-son quest, it also contains a surprising amount about day-to-day activism in relatively organised civic contexts. It ends before he really gets into power but still reads as an extraordinary sequel to Malcolm X's autobiography—the product of enormously expanded opportunities for African-Americans. He works for class justice amongst the very poor but with evident 'resources' that can be mobilised for protest. His own struggle is not for survival but for identity, in pragmatic rather than messianic mode. This quote is from the introduction he wrote to the second edition in 2005, which was reissued when he was 43 and running for Senate:

> I had little time for reflection over the next ten years [after the book first came out]. I ran a voter registration project for the 1992 election cycle, began a civil

rights practice, and started teaching constitutional law at the University of Chicago. My wife and I bought a house, were blessed with two gorgeous, healthy, and mischievous daughters, and struggled to pay the bills. When a seat in the state legislature opened up in 1996, some friends persuaded me to run for the office, and I won. I had been warned, before taking office, that state politics lacks the glamour of its Washington counterpart; one labours largely in obscurity, mostly on topics that mean a great deal to some but that the average man or woman in the street can safely ignore (the regulation of mobile homes, say, or the tax consequences of farm equipment depreciation). Nonetheless, I found the work satisfying, mostly because the scale of state politics allows for concrete results. (viii)

For much of his memoir, Obama portrays himself to be an alienated intellectual alone on the street corner, watching his discarded housing-rights leaflets whirl away in the autumn wind. But, without doubt, his is a consenting dissenting voice that reflects not just the preoccupations of mid-life but a wider course of political opportunity that is distinct for his generation, even for his race. And of course, this autobiography helped him to win the White House, crystallising a 'narrative capital' that theorists now argue to be as important to political success as money or education. However, in the light of the US midterm elections and ongoing critiques of his presidency, it remains to be seen how powerful narrative capital is in the face of the daily reality of politics and whether Obama can regain momentum as he seeks a second term.

Conclusion: Consent and/versus Dissent

It would be easy to deconstruct 'dissent' and find 'consent' within, or even to poke fun at a romantic fantasy of outsider voices. A more serious project is to relate the fascinating tensions within activists' personal writings across their life course to the very real and life-long challenges that face anyone who commits themselves to political change. 'Political process' theories now elaborate many variables that can predict success or failure of social movements, including the degree of openness of the local political system, electoral instability, the availability of influential allies, and tolerance for protest among the elite. The 'political process' approach has succeeded in shifting attention towards inter-actions between new and traditional actors and between less conventional forms of action and institutionalised systems of interest representation. It is thus no longer possible to define movements as *always* marginal and anti-institutional, or as expressions of dysfunctions of the system (Della Porta and Diani 16–7).[4] Activists' life writings trace this evolution of more complex forms of dissent as moderates correspond with radicals and as late-life radicals review their earlier, differently cast struggles. And they also show that activism has profound consequences for the individuals themselves, often disrupting conventional 'life course' patterns that predict a steady sequence of school, employment, marriage and children. This is not how it was—or is—for many of those who came of age in the social movements of the 1960s and 1970s, and their own alternative ageings can be counted as an unintended, but important, consequence of those movements (Giugni).

I want to end with one final example of the imbrications of consent and dissent. David Lewis interviewed mid-life professional activists who have worked in 'non-governmental' organisations but also in governments over the last 20 years. He found that the boundary between working for social change outside government and inside is extremely significant not just for people's sense of themselves but for development policy within and between governments. But because he used a life history method of interviewing, which tracked people's long-term experiences and subjectivities, he was also able to see how fluid that boundary is in practice. People's stories show them going back and forth, often working simultaneously on both sides. Lewis interviewed activists in the Philippines, Bangladesh and the UK, and the very different configurations of politics in each further nuances simple understandings of being 'inside' or 'outside'. In the Philippines, democracy activists in opposition were suddenly offered jobs when their government came into power. Some loved it, but not all of them; many left to go back to lobbying. In the UK, the New Labour government of 1997 brought in voluntary or charitable advisors on temporary secondments as part of a new ideology of 'partnership' government, again with mixed results. But in Bangladesh, it goes the other way: civil servants are often desperate to get out of a badly paid and red-taped government job into the lucrative and often more politically powerful NGO sector. Lewis's sensitive 'life-work' life histories illuminate complex motivations—not just about job security but also perspectives on where change really can take place. Sometimes crossing the boundary—in whichever direction—releases political creativity and personal learning. Sometimes it disappoints.

Lewis concludes that partnerships between those inside and outside formal political institutions are highly politically effective. Here is not the place to assess this. Rather, I would like to conclude by saying more simply that life history interviews can help to show the fluid relationship between dissent and consent that I have been trying to draw out in the analysis of life writings. I hope that with social movement theory and life course theory, such texts across discipline can nuance our ideals of dissenting voices. Perhaps narratives that explain how dissent works alongside consent will prove the most politically revealing in the end. They may also facilitate how we write about activism in our old age.

Notes

[1]   Henderson also explores two startling exceptions, Robin Morgan and Betty Friedan's memoirs, as symptoms of the more forgiving context of American celebrity culture, where these two 'leaders' are less conflicted about their individual success. Margaret Henderson, 'The Feminine Mystique of Individualism Is Powerful: Two American Feminist Memoirs in Postfeminist Times.' *a/b: Auto/Biography Studies* 23.2 (2008). Mary Eberstadt's *Why I Turned Right: Leading Baby Boom Conservatives*

Chronicle Their Political Journeys provides a further contrast, not only because of the dramatic difference in political trajectory but because of the structure of a second conversion narrative.

[2]   See Grey, Sandra and Marian Sawer. 2008.

[3]   For a definition of 'life-course', see Scott, John, and Gordon Marshall. 2009. See also *Oxford Reference Online*.

[4]   Interestingly, Judith Butler speaks in similar terms when she argues that universities need to be allowed to dissent from the State: 'In the context of civil or political disobedience, the impetus for withdrawing one's consent from a given authority consists in trying to establish a limit to governability. [...] But it is not a question of how not to be governed at all'. Butler, Judith. 'Critique, Dissent, Disciplinarity.' *Critical Inquiry* 35 Summer (2009): 791.

References

Ali, Tariq. *Street Fighting Years: An Autobiography of the Sixties*. London: Verso, 2005.

Alibhai-Brown, Yasmin. *No Place Like Home*. London: Virago Press, 1995.

Andrews, Molly. *Lifetimes of Commitment: Aging, Politics and Psychology*. Cambridge: Cambridge University Press, 1991.

Benjamin, Lois. *Three Black Generations at the Crossroads: Community, Culture, and Consciousness*. 2nd ed. Lanham, MD: Rowman & Littlefield, 2007.

Bornat, Joanna, ed *Reminiscence Reviewed: Perspectives, Evaluations, Achievements*. Buckingham: Open University Press, 1994.

Butler, Judith. 'Critique, Dissent, Disciplinarity.' *Critical Inquiry* 35 Summer (2009): 773–97.

Coxsedge, Joan. *Cold Tea for Brandy: A Tale of Protest, Painting and Politics*. Balwyn North, Victoria: Vulcan Press, 2007.

Davies, James C. 'Towards a Theory of Revolution.' *American Sociological Review* 27 (1962): 5–18.

Della Porta, Donatella, and Mario Diani. *Social Movements: An Introduction*. 2nd ed. Malden, MA: Blackwell, 2006.

Eberstadt, Mary. *Why I Turned Right: Leading Baby Boom Conservatives Chronicle Their Political Journeys*. New York: Threshold Editions, 2007.

Erikson, Erik H. Identity and the Life Cycle. London: Norton and Co, 1980. Print.

Egri, Carolyn P., and David A. Ralston. 'Generation Cohorts and Personal Values: A Comparison of China and the U.S.' *Organization Science* 15.2 (2004): 210–20.

Felski, Rita. 'The Doxa of Difference.' *Signs* 23.1 (1997): 1–70.

Gallop, Jane. *Feminist Accused of Sexual Harassment*. Durham, NC: Duke University Press, 1997.

Giugni, Marco G. 'Personal and Biographical Consequences.' *The Blackwell Companion to Social Movements*. Ed. David A. SnowSnow, Sarah Anne Soule, and Hanspeter Kriesi. Oxford: Blackwell, 2004: 489–507.

Grey, Sandra, and Marian Sawer. *Women's Movements: Flourishing or in Abeyance*. Oxford and New York: Oxford University Press, 2008.

Gurr, Ted Robert. *Why Men Rebel*. Princeton: published for the Center of International Studies, Princeton University, 1970.

Henderson, Margaret. 'The Feminine Mystique of Individualism Is Powerful: Two American Feminist Memoirs in Postfeminist Times.' *a/b: Auto/Biography Studies* 23.2 (2008): 165–84.

———. *Marking Feminist Times: Remembering the Longest Revolution in Australia*. Bern: Peter Lang, 2006.

Jay, Karla. *Tales of the Lavender Menace: A Memoir of Liberation.* 1st ed. New York: Basic Books, 1999.

Jolly, Margaretta. *In Love and Struggle: Letters in Contemporary Feminism.* Gender and Culture. New York: Columbia University Press, 2008.

———. 'Three Ways to End a Relationship: Letter Writing and the Dialectics of Political Separatism.' *Last Letters.* Ed. Sylvie Crinquand. Cambridge: Cambridge Scholars Press, 2008: 111–25.

Klein, Naomi. *No Logo: No Space, No Choice, No Jobs.* 10th anniversary ed. London: Fourth Estate, 2010.

Lewis, David. 'Using Life Histories in Social Policy Research: The Case of Third Sector/ Public Sector Boundary Crossing.' *Journal of Social Policy* 37.4 (2008): 1–20.

Melucci, Alberto, John Keane, and Paul Mier. *Nomads of the Present: Social Movements and Individual Needs in Contemporary Society.* London: Hutchinson Radius, 1989.

Obama, Barack. *Dreams from My Father: A Story of Race and Inheritance.* [New] ed. Edinburgh: Canongate, 2007.

Oberschall, Anthony. *Social Conflict and Social Movements.* Englewood Cliffs, NJ: Prentice-Hall, 1973.

Prosser, Jay. *Second Skins: The Body Narratives of Transsexuality.* Gender and Culture. New York: Columbia University Press, 1998.

Roberts, Michele. *Paper Houses: A Memoir of the '70s and Beyond.* London: Virago, 2007.

Rowbotham, Sheila. *Promise of a Dream: Remembering the Sixties.* London: Penguin Books, 2001.

Scott, John, and Gordon Marshall. *A Dictionary of Sociology.* Oxford: Oxford University Press, 2009.

Scott, John, and Gordon Marshall. *Oxford Reference Online.* Accessed November 2010 <http://www.oxfordreference.com/views/ENTRY.html? subview=Main&entry=t88.e126>. Oxford: Oxford University Press.

Segal, Lynne. *Making Trouble: Life and Politics.* London: Serpent's Tail, 2007.

———. 'Who Do You Think You Are? Feminist Memoir Writing.' *New Formations* 67 (2009): 120–33.

Smelser, Neil Joseph. *Theory of Collective Behavior.* London: Routledge & Kegan Paul, 1962.

Spacks, Patricia Meyer. 'Stages of Self: Notes on Autobiography and the Life Cycle.' *Autobiography: Concepts in Literary and Cultural Studies.* Boston University Journal 25 (1977). Ed. Trev Lynn Broughton. Vol. 1. London: Routledge, 2007: 199–212.

Tarrow, Sidney G. *Power in Movement: Social Movements, Collective Action, and Politics.* Cambridge: Cambridge University Press, 1994.

Tilly, Charles. *Stories, Identities, and Political Change.* Lanham, MD: Rowman & Littlefield, 2002.

Touraine, Alain. *The Voice and the Eye: An Analysis of Social Movements.* Cambridge: Cambridge University Press, 1981.

Whitbourne, Susan Krauss, and Sherry L. Willis. *The Baby Boomers Grow Up: Contemporary Perspectives on Midlife.* Mahwah, NJ: Lawrence Erlbaum, 2006.

Williams, Donna. *Nobody Nowhere: The Extraordinary Autobiography of an Autistic.* New York: Avon, 1992.

X, Malcolm, and Alex Haley. *The Autobiography of Malcolm X.* London: Penguin, 2001, 1965.

Detention, Displacement and Dissent in Recent Australian Life Writing

Michael Jacklin

Narratives of persecution, imprisonment, displacement and exile have been a fundamental aspect of Australian literature: from the convict narratives of the eighteenth and nineteenth centuries, to writing by refugees and migrants to Australia following World War II, to the narratives of those displaced by more recent conflicts. This paper will focus on two texts published in Australia in the past few years which deal with experiences of persecution and displacement from Afghanistan. *Mahboba's Promise* (2005) and *The Rugmaker of Mazar-e-Sharif* (2008) are texts that have to some extent bypassed the quarantining that Gillian Whitlock has argued works to locate potentially disruptive discourse at a safe distance from mainstream consumption. The publications discussed here demonstrate that refugee narratives can negotiate their way into the public sphere and public consciousness. In this process, however, representations of dissent almost necessarily give way to conciliation and integration as former refugee subjects attempt to realign their lives in terms that will provide the best outcomes for themselves, their families and their communities.

In June 2010, two months prior to the Australian federal election, the community advocacy group GetUp! gained significant media coverage for refugee issues when it made the winning eBay bid for a surfing lesson with Australian Federal Opposition Leader, Tony Abbott, and then donated that lesson to former Afghan refugee, Riz Wakil. The novelty of a former refugee learning to surf with Tony Abbott, whose hard-line policies on illegally-arrived migrants and potential asylum seekers included a return to the Howard government policy of mandatory detention, proved irresistible to the media. Over the next several weeks, the story resulted in more than 50 interviews and $500,000 worth of media exposure. By late July, GetUp! had raised over $130,000 to support the broadcast of an advertisement featuring Wakil speaking direct to camera, addressing Tony Abbott in advance of his surf lesson:

> Mr Abbott, if you heard the stories of real refugees, you would know that tougher policies would not keep them from coming. Your approach will just bring them more pain. I had to flee Afghanistan when I was just eighteen, after my brother was kidnapped. I risked my life on a dangerous journey. There was no safe way to safety. Then I was locked up in Curtin Detention Centre, where I saw many terrible things. Now I'm a small business owner, a proud Australian and I look forward to meeting you Mr Abbott, to share my story and the stories of other refugees. Please Mr Abbott, listen to our stories. Make your policies more humane. (GetUp!)[1]

The return of refugee issues to public debate in the lead-up to, and over the course of, the 2010 Australian federal election is not surprising. In 2008, the Labor government had ended the previous Coalition government's policies of mandatory detention, Temporary Protection Visas and the 'Pacific Solution'. Mandatory detention had resulted in thousands of asylum seekers held in detention centres, some for years, generating significant public protest, particularly in regard to children held in detention. Temporary Protection Visas allowed for a three year period of protection, with the need for protection then reassessed and asylum seekers returned to their country of origin if it were deemed safe to do so. The 'Pacific Solution' saw unauthorised arrivals transferred to offshore processing centres on Nauru and Manus Island, where claims for asylum were processed outside the jurisdiction of Australian law and claimants were ineligible for legal assistance or for judicial review. In the period during which these policies were in place, arrivals of boats carrying illegal migrants to Australia had fallen significantly, from more than 40 or 50 boats per year to less than 10. In 2009, however, arrivals rose again to 59 boats for the year, with that same number arriving in just the first five months of 2010 (Boat Arrivals). In April 2009, an explosion on a boat carrying Afghan asylum seekers to Australian waters killed five asylum seekers. In October, Australian Customs rescued 78 Sri Lankans from a disabled boat and returned them to Indonesian waters, leading to a month-long period of negotiation with the refugees who refused to leave the Australian ship. And in July 2010, with a change in Australian Prime Ministers and an election looming, the Labor government announced that it would begin negotiations with East Timor for the establishment of a regional refugee processing centre, a proposal seen by some as being Labor's version of the Coalition's Pacific Solution (Coorey, p.1).[2]

Refugee issues have been a factor in every Australian election over the past 10 years. What is significant about Riz Wakil's media appearance is that by speaking directly to a viewing and a reading audience, as well as to the leader of the opposition, Wakil thus gives a name and face to a debate often overwhelmed by statistics, or by images of degradation, violence and self-harm.[3] In *Soft Weapons: Autobiography in Transit* (2007), Gillian Whitlock argues that such personalisation is rare in refugee discourse. She makes the point that '[d]ehumanizing the figure of the asylum seeker, denying the human referent of face and body at all costs, is a response to threat: unwelcome strangers endanger the integrity of the nation'(73). Whitlock notes that there have been very few book-length biographies or autobiographies of recent refugees to Australia. In *Soft Weapons*, her analysis of refugee life writing focuses on the highly mediated, highly controlled textual platforms through which refugee narratives and testimony most frequently enter public circulation: activist and human rights websites such as those of Human Rights Watch, Amnesty International or anthologies edited and compiled with the support of groups such as PEN. She argues, however, that the testimony circulating in this way risks achieving little public impact: 'To accrue value and jurisdiction, testimony needs fortune, history and national interest on its side. Asylum seekers have none of these things' (79). Of greater impact, she claims, has been the strategy of adopting a 'wound culture' in which detained asylum seekers 'write graffiti in blood, carve words on skin, and speak with sutured lips' (83). Relatively few Australians will have sought or read the refugee narratives appearing in publications Whitlock cites, yet anyone watching the news in those same years will remember images of refugees with lips sewn together. For Whitlock, this too is testimony. She terms such acts of protest 'testimony incarnate' and argues that this performative testimony of 'disgust and hate and shame'(85) confronts the viewer/reader in ways that narrative imagination cannot and does so with a force which 'produces a shattering sense of the limits of our own self and its place to speak humanely' (86).

Riz Wakil's autobiographical presence is not of this shattering kind. It is worth noting that Wakil's story first appeared in the discourse surrounding refugee lives through one of the anthologies that Whitlock cites. In *Dark Dreams: Australian Refugee Stories by Young Writers, Aged 11–20 Years* (2004), 14-year-old writer Zac Darab bases his story, 'From a Small Detention Centre, I Am Now in a Bigger Detention Centre: The Story of an Afghan Refugee', on conversations with Wakil, who at the time had been released from Curtin Detention Centre, at first on a Temporary Protection Visa, and later with a Permanent Residency Visa. Darab recounts Wakil's journey from Afghanistan to Australia, his experiences in detention and his life in Australia following release. Wakil's story in this publication was one among the many fragments of refugee narratives that, Whitlock argues, entered the public sphere through the efforts of advocacy groups. Whitlock emphasises, however, that despite the intentions of those involved—the advocates, editors, narrators and writers—these fragments of refugee and asylum seeker lives had little impact on the national psyche. Refugee stories in this form, Whitlock maintains, 'continue to languish on the margins of the public sphere' (76).

Wakil's story, however, has not languished. In fact, his story has appeared repeatedly in Australian media, beginning in 2003, again in 2004, in 2006 and now in 2010.[4] While his narrative is frequently associated with the public campaigns of advocacy groups, it is also, nevertheless, a refugee narrative very much embodied and is one that has accrued some degree of familiarity in Australian consciousness. His story is one of displacement and of detention; his voice is one of dissent—not desperate, shocking or shaming, but reasonable and personable, seeking an empathetic engagement of the sort that Whitlock argues has had little impact. Whitlock may well be right, but what I would like to do in this essay is to examine two recent examples of Australian life writing texts that offer book-length accounts of the experiences of those who have fled repression in their countries of origin. As previously noted, when Whitlock was writing *Soft Weapons*, there were very few monographs of refugee experiences relating to this most recent period of conflict and displacement. Certainly, numerous autobiographies and biographies have been published narrating the lives of those who came to Australia as refugees from Europe following World War II. There is also a significant body of auto/biographical narratives associated with the Vietnam War and Vietnamese refugees, many of whom settled in Australia. The recent years of conflict in Afghanistan, Iraq and Iran, however, have generated far fewer book-length autobiographical accounts by displaced people from that region who have come to Australia. There are, however, a handful of notable texts, and I would like to discuss two of these in some detail, as they illustrate a range of issues relating to the narration of dissent and its consequences. Both are first-person autobiographical narratives written with the assistance of a profes-sional writer. Therefore, the discursive constraints of collaborative textual production, as Whitlock insists in her analysis of refugee narratives, will warrant consideration in the discussion which follows.

Published in 2005, *Mahboba's Promise* provides a first-person account of events in Soviet-occupied Afghanistan of the 1980s. Although not a refugee narrative from the most recent round of violence and displacement, Mahboba Rawi's book appeared at a time when the Australian media were devoting considerable attention to Afghanistan. Rawi's book was the first in Australia to offer a personal account by a woman displaced from Afghanistan by conflict, albeit the conflict experienced by an earlier generation. The first half of the book focuses on the circumstances leading to the narrator's involvement in student protests in Kabul and her eventual experience of displacement in Pakistan. In the Australian-located second half, the narrative develops into one of migrant integration as Rawi struggles to overcome the challenges of adapting to a new culture and then personal loss and grief. In 1992, events in Rawi's life intersected with the Australian media following a family tragedy at Kiama on the south coast of New South Wales, when seven members of Sydney's Afghan migrant community were swept into the sea at the Blowhole, a well-known tourist attraction in the area. One of the victims was seven-year-old Arash, Rawi's son, who had gone sight-seeing that day with his aunt, uncle and cousin, all of whom were drowned. Rawi herself was not present and does not feature in the media reporting of the time, but she does appear in the media in 2001, when ABC Television's *7.30 Report* covered her involvement with English language pro-grammes for Afghan women in Sydney and her fund-raising for Afghan orphans in refugee camps in Pakistan. In 2002, she appeared on ABC Television's *Australian Story*, leading a group of Australian women into refugee camps in Pakistan and into Afghanistan to draw attention to her ongoing fund-raising efforts for women and children affected by the war (Masters). This broadcast resulted in a huge increase in donations and volunteers for her aid organisation called Mahboba's Promise. In 2009, Rawi was back on the *7.30 Report*, again to raise awareness of the difficulties faced by Afghan women and orphans and to maintain support for her organisation (Haussegger). Rawi's public presence and the reputation of her work is such that in January 2009, when Australian Governor-General Quentin Bryce made a secret two-day visit to Afghanistan to speak to Australian troops there, she found time to visit the Mahboba's Promise orphanage in Kabul (Dodd). The point I wish to emphasise is that Rawi's story is another example of a refugee narrative that, far from languishing on the margins of the public sphere, has had significant and tangible social impact, changing the lives of Afghans who are receiving health, housing and educational assistance, and the lives of Australians who have been encouraged to volunteer and become involved in the circumstances and well-being of refugees. The book *Mahboba's Promise* has not, on its own, achieved this but is an integral part of this discursive network of circulation and narrative exchange.

But what role does dissent play in Rawi's story? It is important to point out that Rawi did not come to Australia as a refugee, although it *was* as a refugee that she had fled Afghanistan, and she identifies herself throughout her narrative as a displaced person. Unlike Afghan refugees who arrived in Australia in the period following 2000, Rawi came here in the mid-1980s as a migrant, having married another Afghan who had Australian residency. In the years leading up to this, however, Rawi had lived as a refugee in Pakistan, having been forced to flee Kabul after being targeted for arrest by security forces. The opening chapters of *Mahboba's Promise* detail these circumstances, leading to the narrator's decision to leave. During her years as a high-school student, Rawi became active in the student protest movement, painting banners with anti-Russian slogans (35), burning communist books from the school library (48) and forming links with protestors from other schools. Rawi's name was revealed to security forces and, on the same day, a crackdown at her school resulted in more students being taken into custody. Rawi escaped and went into hiding, and her family then arranged for her to travel with relatives to Pakistan (56). This section of the book explains both the historical and political forces determining the course of the narrator's life and the formation of her character as she responds to the challenges of living under military occupation as a displaced person. Although dissent has altered the course of her life story, her assertion and determination—her father calls her 'his "sweet lion daughter"' (68)—are the very qualities that will draw others to her cause years later in Australia and lead to her name being included in a list published in *The Age* newspaper of 'The 50 Australians Who Matter' (Dale).[5]

Not all refugee narratives are propelled by acts of dissent. *The Rugmaker of Mazar-e-Sharif* (2008) is the first-person narrative of Najaf Mazari, a Hazara man from Afghanistan. Its narrative provides an account of Mazari's growing up in Afghanistan under the Soviet occupation and mujahedin resistance, and later, during conflict with the Taliban. During the earlier period, Mazari was seriously injured and members of his family were killed when their home was struck in a rocket attack. In the latter period, his city, Mazar-e-Sharif, was the site of a Taliban massacre of the Hazara population.[6] During this violence, Mazari hid in a cupboard for 15 days, and when he emerged, he was captured and imprisoned by the Taliban and tortured (196–202). Throughout the years of upheaval in Afghanistan, the persecution which Mazari and his family experienced had no connection with dissent or protest. Their plight results solely from their ethnicity. The narrative reveals that throughout his life, Mazari has opted to avoid dissent wherever possible. His attitude is made clear early in the book when he relates a traditional story of an old camel and its son. The young camel was given to complaining until one day the old camel counsels the younger to look up towards the mountains ahead. 'Come what may, we must climb those mountains. If you lament now, what will be left when the real work begins?' (99). Later, when Mazari is in Australia, he refers to the story again in order to emphasise his self-control and determination to fit in (187). In Afghanistan, however, with his life in danger, Mazari and his family see no choice but for him to flee. He explains their reasoning in paying a people-smuggler to arrange his escape and his travel to Australia: 'if the family tribe cannot survive, then by mercy of God, let one male member of that tribe find safety in the world, and let him rebuild everything from the start' (221).

The Rugmaker of Mazar-e-Sharif is structured in alternating chapters, moving between Mazari's life in Afghanistan and in Australia, where he is held in Woomera Detention Centre until he is granted a Temporary Protection Visa, followed by his attempts to establish a life in Australia as a rug mender. The narrative is remarkable for being one of the few book-length autobiographical accounts, published thus far, of life inside Australia's detention centres.[7] The book, in fact, opens with Mazari imprisoned in Woomera and singing a song in Dari to console himself in his sorrow and loneliness. Guards hear his song and an interpreter asks him to sing it again. Mazari recounts:

> [I]t strikes me that all the words I had employed in my long interview with the immigration officer and everything I have said to the officers and guards since, have not made a fraction of the impact on them as my song. For a few minutes, I was not merely one of hundreds of down-at-heel nuisances from some hellhole in Central Asia, but a man with something to offer, a song to sing and maybe a tale to tell that might be worth listening to; a tale that might even be true. (5)

Mazari's account of life in Woomera is signalled here as one that will provide insight into refugee and detainee lives in ways that interviews and statistics and reports cannot. In recounting the joy he felt at singing in Dari, he says, 'It is a pleasure to use my native tongue in this way, exploring the shadows of language. There is very little poetry to enjoy during a normal day in camp' (4). The implication is that the narrative to follow will be one marked by lyricism, an odd trait to associate with refugee testimony and a pole apart from the testimony incarnate which Whitlock asserts produces a shattering sense of the limits of self and one's place to speak humanely. Like Riz Wakil, with whom this essay opened, Najaf Mazari offers a narrative characterised by reasonableness, one that draws on Afghan song and parable and traditional story, and one that draws its readers gently, personably, into the daily experiences of detention. Whereas contemporary media coverage emphasised the violence and degradation of detention, Mazari chooses to think of Woomera as a school in which one can learn what is expected of a good refugee: good manners, respecting queues, eating without complaint, not appearing pushy (68–71). Although in part this is intended ironically, Mazari is also narrating his own strategies for surviving detention. Progressing with relative ease from the intake camp to Main Camp, where he awaits the processing of his claim, Mazari entertains his readers with narratives of unrequited love amongst the detainees, tales not dissimilar in style to the traditional stories of his youth. Although Mazari hears of events in Sierra Camp, where reputedly the trouble-makers are held, and he witnesses violent protest, including an inmate's sewing together of his own lips, his commentary focuses predominantly on conciliation. *The Rugmaker of Mazar-e-Sharif* is, then, the story of a refugee learning to cope and adapt, with dissent playing little part in this narrative of a dislocated life. It is not surprising that the book ends with the trope of integration, as Mazari attends a ceremony at Malvern Town Hall in Melbourne where he receives his Australian citizenship. Again, reasonableness is underscored, with Mazari pointing out that to become Australian he was not asked to 'tell the world that Australia is the best country on earth', or 'to make myself ready to fight people in the streets with an automatic rifle' or 'to say that I loved the Prime Minister. I was asked only to obey the laws of Australia, and I gladly agreed to that' (252).

Unlike Mahboba Rawi, Najaf Mazari had no media profile prior to his narrative being published. After his release from Woomera, Mazari found work repairing Afghan rugs and eventually was able to open his own shop in Melbourne. Through his shop, his circle of Australian acquaintances grew, with a friend eventually introducing him to Iris Breuer and Cathi Lewis of Insight Publications who, '(a)fter many get-togethers over Afghani food and cardamom tea,' commissioned author Robert Hillman to write Mazari's story (255). Insight Publications is a Melbourne-based company producing educational texts and resources aimed mainly at the upper-secondary school level. They promote *The Rugmaker of Mazar-e-Sharif* as a non-fiction text ideal for years 9 to 12 and provide an accompanying study guide, also written by Hillman. Mazari and Hillman have appeared at book readings, a literacy conference and writers' festivals and their book has received positive reviews across a range of Australian media.[8] I want to suggest, then, that in spite of Mazari's prior lack of media presence, book publication has resulted in some degree of mainstream attention, making his another case of a refugee narrative managing to achieve circulation and to potentially impact upon public consciousness.[9]

An important qualification to the argument developed throughout this essay that refugee narratives have in some cases moved from the margins to the mainstream is the matter of mediation and discursive constraint. The narratives of disrupted lives discussed here have each entered the market through the efforts, or with the assistance of, interested others who mediate between narrating subjects and their readers. These writing partners do, indeed, as Whitlock asserts, 'shepherd' the narratives along mostly familiar paths to publication (57). Hillman's involvement in the writing of *The Rugmaker of Mazar-e-Sharif* is particularly illustrative. Hillman is a distinguished autobiographer, with his 2005 memoir *The Boy in the Green Suit* winning the National Biography Award. He is also the author of non-fiction books for young readers. As well, by coincidence or not, he is the co-author of another autobiographical account of detention.[10] *My Life as a Traitor* (2007), by Iranian-born and now Australian resident, Zarah Ghahramani and Hillman, is an account of Ghahramani's imprisonment in Tehran's Evin Prison. Like *The Rugmaker of Mazar-e-Sharif*, *My Life as a Traitor* is structured with dual time-frames, with alternating present-tense, past-tense chapters. Whereas Mazari's narrative moves between his experiences of detention and then settlement in Australia and the circumstances in Afghanistan that forced him to become an asylum seeker, Ghahramani's narrative shifts between her experiences of detention and torture in Iran and the circumstances of her life in Tehran that led to her arrest. The most glaring contrast between the two books is that *My Life as a Traitor* has no Australian content at all. The only indication of an Australian connection is a mention on the back cover that the co-author Robert Hillman 'befriended Zarah in Iran in 2003 and helped her escape to Australia, where she now has permanent residency'. Since its Australian publication, her book has been published in America and Europe and translated into at least four other languages, becoming one of the many texts of Iranian dissent circulating internationally. Mazari's book, on the other hand, with its account of life in Woomera and resettlement in Melbourne, is likely to remain limited to its Australian publication. The point I want to make with this comparison is perhaps the obvious one that the writing partner's contribution to the ultimate form of the narrative and its potential to enter particular markets is substantial. Whitlock, in this regard, is quite right, and an awareness of the circumstances of mediation should be integral to reading and reflecting upon refugee lives.[11]

Whether the mediating process is considered constraining or facilitating depends upon one's focus, or one's critical perspective. Amongst the refugee narratives and testimony that interest Whitlock in *Soft Weapons*, mediation results in a type of quarantining, a locating of disruptive discourse at a safe distance from mainstream consumption. The book-length narratives surveyed here demonstrate that refugee narratives can negotiate their way into the public sphere. In doing so, however, dissent almost necessarily gives way to conciliation and integration as former refugee subjects attempt to realign their lives in terms that will provide the best outcomes for themselves and their families. This concern for outcomes extends as well to the narrators' communities of origin. *Mahboba's Promise*, in particular, devotes a substantial portion of its narrative to the performance of good works, as its narrator, after the death of her child and the break-up of her marriage, turns her life around by studying Islam and devoting herself to helping others (162–7). Both *Mahboba's Promise* and *The Rugmaker of Mazar-e-Sharif*, in their final pages, provide directions to associated websites where readers can learn more and can volunteer or donate towards programmes assisting communities in Afghanistan. The thought that a book published in Australia telling the story of a former refugee might generate sufficient interest to impact on disrupted lives halfway around the world might seem far-fetched, but both Rawi and Mazari continue to be active in fund-raising and public awareness events, and their books continue to circulate.[12] Whether refugee narratives have a wider effect on the public debate in Australia regarding refugees and detention is, of course, open to question, yet the fact that these stories are read in book groups, that their authors speak at writers' festivals, film openings and other public events is a substantial change in the writing and circulation of refugee life writing in Australia.

Notes

[1] 'The video is now on youtube at http://www.youtube.com/watch?v=dW5CdVXb XMM&feature=youtu.be There is a link to this youtube clip from the GetUp! site at https://www.getup.org.au/campaigns/fair-go/children-out-of-detention/children-out-of-detention This means that the URL for GetUp! in mylist of references should be changed to this new one. See 12/50']

[2] Since submitting this article, refugee issues have continued to make headlines in Australia, the most tragic event being the shipwreck of an asylum seeker vessel at Christmas Island in December 2010, with over 50 people drowning. In April 2011, during protests by detainees at Villawood Detention Centre, nine buildings were seriously damaged by fire. In May, the government announced its plan to exchange asylum seekers already in Australia for refugees awaiting resettlement in Malaysia. Also in May 2011, Riz Wakil finally received his surfing lesson with Tony Abbott (see Wright and O'Rourke).

[3] Compare Wakil's media presence to that of other former refugees such as Parviz Yousefi, the Iranian refugee who was among detainees at Woomera Detention Centre who sewed their lips together and joined in a hunger strike in protest at their treatment. In 2005, Yousefi lodged a claim with the New South Wales (NSW) Supreme Court for compensation for wages and medical care owing to the psychiatric damage he had suffered in detention. Newspaper articles covering the 2008 success of his claim reported that he was 'too sick to comment' (Murphy, p.4).

[4] See Stephen, Maley, Patty, and Harrison respectively. The media reports by Maley and Patty are cited in Helf, who provides a discussion of Wakil's narrative, as written by Darab and appearing in *Dark Dreams*.

[5] Dale compiled his list of 50 Australians who matter based on an assessment of the impact they have had on others lives and on an understanding that 'the world would be a different place without them'. His list includes prominent business people, communicators, entertainers, scientists and 'helpers', with Rawi included in the latter category. Again, this supports my contention that refugee lives and narratives are not always consigned to the margins of the public sphere.

[6] See 'Afghanistan: The Human Rights of Minorities,' pp 4–5 for an account of events of 1998. Amnesty International states that no journalists or independent monitors were allowed into the area but that reports of deaths reached into the thousands.

[7] Other accounts include the biographies *The Bitter Shore* (2008) and *Freeing Ali: The Human Face of the Pacific Solution* (2005), and *Moza's Story, an Ashmore Reef*

Account : Based on a True Story, an assisted autobiographical narrative of 87 pages, with the narrator's identity protected by a pseudonym.

[8] See, for example: Adams; Johnston; and On.

[9] If I can be permitted an anecdote, returning to Australia recently from an overseas trip, I sat next to a woman from Melbourne who, when I enquired whether she'd read any refugee narratives, replied that she knew 'the Afghan rugmaker's book' and spoke enthusiastically of visiting his shop to meet him.

[10] Hillman has written of his involvement with both Mazari and Ghahramani in an article appearing in the *Griffith Review* prior to the publication of these two books. He reveals details of his meeting with Ghahramani but little of how he was approached to work with Mazari and nothing of the writing process for either book.

[11] Circumstances of mediation are, of course, frequently underplayed in the publications. *Mahboba's Promise* is a case in point, with no information provided regarding the co-author, Vanessa Mickan-Gramazio, except in the author's blurb which states that she has a Masters in Writing and has worked as a book editor for 10 years.

[12] As this article is submitted for publication, the Mazari website advertises its annual fundraiser for October 2010, with donations contributing to the purchase of ambulances in northern Afghanistan.

References

Adams, Phillip. 'An Afghan's Tale'. *Late Night Live*. ABC Radio National 17 April 2008. Accessed 10 July 2010, <http://www.abc.net.au/rn/latenightlive/stories/2008/2219899.htm>.

Amnesty International. 'Afghanistan: The Human Rights of Minorities,' AI Index ASA 11/14/99 (November 1999). Accessed 12 July 2010, <http://www.amnesty.org/en/library/asset/ASA11/014/1999/en/43c4282d-e035-11dd-865a-d728958ca30a/asa110141999en.pdf>.

Coorey, Phillip. 'Labor's Indian Ocean Solution.' *Sydney Morning Herald* 7 July 2010. Accessed 10 July 2010, <http://www.smh.com.au/national/labors-indian-ocean-solution-20100706-zz3x.html>.

Dale, David. 'The 50 Australians Who Matter.' *The Age* 22 January 2005. Accessed 28 September 2009, <http://www.theage.com.au/articles/2005/01/20/1106110882796.html>.

Dechian, Sonia, Heather Millar, and Eva Sallis, eds, *Dark Dreams: Australian Refugee Stories by Young Writers, Aged 11–20 Years*. Kent Town, AUS: Wakefield Press, 2004.

Dodd, Mark. 'Governor-General Quentin Bryce Secret Visit to Afghan Base.' *The Australian* 22 January 2009. Accessed 28 September 2009, <http://www.theaustralian.news.com.au/story/0,25197,24945788-25837,00.html>.

Everitt, Jacquie. *The Bitter Shore*. Sydney: Macmillan, 2008.

GetUp! Action for Australia. Children out of Detention. 2010. Accessed on 7 October 2011, <https://www.getup.org.au/campaigns/fair-go/children-out-of-detention/children-out-of-detention>.

Ghahramani, Zarah, with Robert Hillman. *My Life as a Traitor*. Carleton North, Canada: Scribe, 2007.

Gordon, Michael. *Freeing Ali: The Human Face of the Pacific Solution*. Sydney: University of New South Wales Press, 2005.

Harrison, Dan. 'Surf's up for Abbott in GetUp! bid,' The Age 17 June 2010. Accessed 10 July 2010, <http://www.theage.com.au/national/melbourne-life/surfs-up-for-abbott-in-getup-bid-20100616-yggn.html >

Haussegger, Virginia. 'Mahboba's Promise.' *7.30 Report*. Australian Broadcasting Corporation 2 July 2009. Accessed 28 September 2009, <http://www.abc.net.au/7.30/content/2009/s2615472.htm>.

Helf, Sissy. 'Children in Detention: Juvenile Authors Recollect Refugee Stories.' *Papers: Explorations in Children's Literature* 17.2 (2007): 67–74.

Hillman, Robert. *The Boy in the Green Suit: A Memoir*. Carlton North: Scribe, 2003

——. 'Beyond Pity.' *Griffith Review* (Autumn 2007): 211–20.

'The Inside Story: An Inside View of What Is Going on in Detention Centres,' *Four Corners*. Australian Broadcasting Corporation 13 August 2001. Accessed 30 September 2009, <http://www.abc.net.au/4corners/stories/s344246.htm>.

Johnston, Tim. 'One Man's Journey a Tale of Our Times.' *The Weekend Australian* 10–11 May 2008: 13.

Maley, Jacqueline. 'The Rights Stuff.' *Sydney Morning Herald* 14 September 2007. Accessed 22 July 2010, <http://www.smh.com.au/articles/2004/06/17/1087245026309.html?from=stories>.

Masters, Deb. 'Crossing the Kyber.' *Australian Story*. Australian Broadcasting Corporation 4 November 2002. Accessed 28 September 2009, <http://www.abc.net.au/austory/transcripts/s715061.htm>.

Mazari, Najaf, and Robert Hillman. *The Rugmaker of Mazar-e-Sharif*. Elsternwick, AUS: Insight Publications, 2008.

Moza, and Emma Stevens. *Moza's Story, an Ashmore Reef Account: Based on a True Story*. Melville, WA: Kaleidoscope, 2005.

Murphy, Damien. 'Record Payout for Refugee Who Sewed Lips.' *Sydney Morning Herald* 12 January 2008. Accessed 24 July 2010, <http://www.smh.com.au/news/national/record-payout-for-refugee/2008/01/11/1199988590128.html>.

On, Thuy. 'Weft and Weave of an Asylum Seeker.' *The Age* 3 May 2008: A2, 23.

Parliament of Australia. Parliamentary Library. 'Boat Arrivals in Australia since 1976.' On-line 25 June 2009, updated 26 May 2010. Accessed 25 July 2010, <http://www.aph.gov.au/library/pubs/bn/sp/BoatArrivals.htm#_Toc233686295>.

Patty, Anna. 'Child Refugees Denied Basic Rights—Study.' *Sydney Morning Herald* 7 August 2006. Accessed 10 July 2010, <http://www.smh.com.au/news/national/child-refugees-denied-basic-rights--study/2006/08/06/1154802756063.html>.

Rawi, Mahboba, and Vanessa Mickan-Gramazio. *Mahboba's Promise: How One Woman Made a World of Difference*. Sydney: Bantam, 2005.

Stephen, Sarah. 'Ruddock's Blackmail: Refugees Robbed of Human Rights.' *Green Left Weekly* 22 January 2003. Accessed 10 July 2010, <http://www.greenleft.org.au/node/28410>.

Whitlock, Gillian. *Soft Weapons: Autobiography in Transit*. Chicago: University of Chicago Press, 2007.

Wright, Jessica, and Jim O'Rourke. 'We'll Stop the … Longboards?' *The Sun-Herald* 8 May 2011: 4.

'The Closet of the Third Person': Susan Sontag, Sexual Dissidence, and Celebrity

Guy Davidson

In this essay I argue that the tension between Susan Sontag's status as a postmodern celebrity and her devotion to the modernist cult of impersonality may be productively related to her sexuality. Beginning with her famous essay 'Notes of Camp' (1964), Sontag aligned herself (somewhat uneasily) with metropolitan gay culture. On the other hand, Sontag was one of the most famous undeclared lesbians in recent history. While she largely eschewed life writing, her fiction, essays, and interviews have often been read by critics for their autobiographical resonances. I extend this critical tendency by attending to the articulation and elision of what Jonathan Dollimore calls sexual dissidence in Sontag's writing. I also reflect on the difference the publication of the first of a series of three projected volumes of her journals makes to our ideas about Sontag and sexuality.

1

The reluctance of the novelist, essayist, and celebrity intellectual Susan Sontag to come out as lesbian or bisexual was, in the decade or so before her death in 2004, one of the most well-known facts about this very well-known individual. Celebrity has been defined as the point at which the public figure engages interest at the level of private life.[1] Celebrities themselves, however, especially queer ones, are often anxious to bar access to information about their erotic lives, and this was very much the case with Sontag. In an interview from the early 1990s, when reporters were starting to ask questions about her sexuality, she stated, 'I don't talk about my erotic life any more than I talk about my spiritual life. It is...too complex and it always ends up sounding so banal' (qtd. in Seligman 102–3). Later she declared rather stuffily, 'indiscretion about one's unconventional sexual feelings is now a routine, if not mandatory, contribution to public entertainment' (*Where the Stress Falls* 104; qtd. in Seligman 103). Only in 2000, when an unauthorised biography detailing her love affairs with women was about to appear, did Sontag pre-emptively half-acknowledge what had by then become an open secret. In an interview in the *New Yorker*, she said: 'That I have had girlfriends as well as boyfriends is what? Is something I never thought I was supposed to say since it seems to me the most natural thing in the world' (qtd. in Seligman 103). The throwaway disingenuousness of the remark is matched by its intellectual shoddiness: the Sontag who in previous years had written bracingly about the cultural meanings of the erotic would hardly have countenanced this airy relegation of 'unconventional sexual feelings' to the realm of the 'natural', that is, the not-worth-mentioning. Moreover, Sontag's brief marriage to the University of Chicago sociologist Philip Rieff, with whom she had a son, David, secured for her for many years a nominal public identity as a heterosexual. And it's not true that she never spoke about her erotic life. Most strikingly, in an interview with *Rolling Stone* from 1978, Sontag speaks at some length on this topic, though in carefully degendered terms (*Conversations* 124–8).

My aim in this essay, however, is neither to upbraid Sontag for her lack of openness, nor to express disappointment that such an influential individual should have proved unwilling to come out earlier and more definitively. Instead, I wish to attend to the elision and articulation of what Jonathan Dollimore calls sexual dissidence in Sontag's work—to suggest some of the ways in which despite, or indeed because of her reticence, queer sexuality centrally informed her career. The term sexual dissidence has taken on a life of its own since Dollimore used it as the title for his wide-ranging 1991 study of the place of homosexuality in Christian and post-Christian culture, carrying as it does the politically useful connotation of active disagreement with heteronormativity. But the examples of active disagreement that Dollimore discusses—like the cultural and textual materials discussed by queer theory generally—tend to operate through subversion rather than open challenge, a mode of dissent necessitated by the severe punishments that have long rained down upon queer people. In the spirit of queer-theoretical enquiry into the possibilities of the subversive text, I want to suggest that the interplay between the disclosure and obfuscation of sexual dissidence in Sontag's work can be connected to various tensions in her career: the tension between modernism and postmodernism, and, related to this, the tension between her espousal of the modernist shibboleth of impersonality and her celebrity status. In particular, I draw upon Eve Kosofsky Sedgwick's claim that 'any aspect of Western culture must be, not merely incomplete, but damaged in its central substance to the degree that it does not incorporate a critical analysis of modern homo/heterosexual definition' (1).

The tendency to read Sontag's essays and fiction as a kind of veiled life writing has become an established approach in studies of her work; indeed, at least insofar as the essays in particular function as kind of intellectual autobiography, this critical tendency was accorded Sontag's own imprimatur. In a prefatory note to *Against Interpretation* (1966), the collection of the essays from the early 1960s with which she made her name, Sontag stated that 'in the end what I have been writing is not criticism at all, strictly speaking, but case studies for an aesthetic, a theory of my own sensibility' (viii). Later, in an essay on Walter Benjamin from 1978, Sontag wrote, 'One cannot use the life to interpret the work. But one can use the work to interpret the life' (*Under the Sign of Saturn* 111); and critics have deployed this aperçu as a license to probe Sontag's work for its autobiographical resonances. Sontag herself noted in a 1984 interview that her essays on Benjamin, Elias Canetti, and Roland Barthes were 'portraits that are in some sense self-portraits' (*Conversations* 208). On the other hand, in 'Singleness', an essay from 1995, she repudiated psychologising interpretations, stating, 'my books are not a means of discovering who I am either; I've never fancied the ideology of writing as therapy or self-expression' (*Where the Stress Falls* 260). But the first person always hovered tantalisingly behind the usually third-person mode of Sontag's expression—as her own statements indicate, acknowledging and then withdrawing the first-person presence in a kind of *fort/da* game with her readers.

In what follows, I draw upon and extend the critical tendency to use Sontag's 'work to interpret the life', juxtaposing a reading of the essays— in particular those collected in *Against Interpretation* and especially 'Notes on Camp'—with a reading of *Reborn*, a recently published selection from Sontag's journals and notebooks, the first volume of a projected three. If in her essays Sontag implicitly and self-reflexively raises the possibility of an autobiographical reading of a prose famous for its impersonality, what difference does it make that we now have available the journals in which the first person, rather than being covertly expressed, dramatically emerges? Covering the period from 1947 to 1963—from her adolescence in Los Angeles to her early years in New York, where she began to establish herself as a writer—*Reborn* is unstintingly frank about her erotic relations with women and her identification as a lesbian, providing a near-shocking contrast to the reticence with which she treated her sexual life in her public utterances. On the most obvious level, the journals begin to provide the missing piece of the puzzle that Sontag herself withheld, enabling an understanding of the sexual and sentimental autobiography to put alongside the intellectual autobiography that may be gleaned from her essays and interviews. But I want to suggest that the sexual—more specifically, the *homosexual*—and the intellectual were entwined in Sontag's published work from the beginning. While the journals provide an invaluable resource for thinking through the difference Sontag's sexuality made to her career, I am not primarily interested in the extent to which the journals round out our understanding of her sexual identity; rather, I read the indirect life writing of the essays in juxtaposition with the life writing proper of the journals in order to parse the persistence as well as the changes in the interrelation of celebrity, self-conception, and sexuality in Sontag's life and work.

2

Against Interpretation is often regarded as championing the new modes of art and aesthetic appreciation collected under the rubric 'postmodernism'.

Alongside essays on established figures such as Albert Camus and Georg Lukács, the book includes celebrations of such avatars of what Sontag called 'the new sensibility' as Jean-Luc Godard, Nathalie Sarraute, and—several rungs down the ladder of cultural respectability—science-fiction movies, and Jack Smith's *Flaming Creatures* (1963), the New York underground film banned for shots of nudity and masturbation. It has rightly been pointed out that Sontag's investment in unsanctioned and popular forms of culture has been overstated, as Sontag was primarily a champion of the rigors of modernism. Nevertheless, the challenges she issued to the entrenched devotion to high culture that characterised mid-twentieth-century US intellectual life formed an indelible aspect of her public image, despite her tendency, as her career progressed, to emphasise the importance of artistic canons and intellectual seriousness.

Sontag also seems aligned with the postmodern in her status as a much-photographed celebrity—her participation in what Fredric Jameson describes in his well-known definition of postmodernity as 'a whole new culture of the image or the simulacrum' (6). If Sontag declined to make explicit her sexual dissidence, her persona was, due to these ubiquitous images of her striking beauty, highly sexualised—in 1967, in a passage from his memoir *Making It*, to which I'll return, Norman Podhoretz dubbed her the 'Dark Lady of American Letters'. But Sontag disavowed her own participation in the postmodern mediascape and her own celebrity status. She actually denounced the pervasiveness of photography in her book-length essay *On Photography* (1977) and the pervasiveness of TV unrelentingly in interviews throughout her career. With regard to her mass media fame, in an interview with Richard Bernstein from 1989 she insisted, 'My life is entirely private. My interests are not those of a pop celebrity', but that 'still, the legend' of her active pursuit of publicity 'goes on'. Sontag disavows the actuality that in the late twentieth century the status of celebrity can extend not only to pop-culture figures but also to novelists and intellectuals.

Also in tension with her much-photographed and much-interviewed presence, Sontag claimed, as a writer, to be more interested in self-transcendence than in self-expression. Both her fiction and the work of the writers and thinkers she promoted in her essays share concerns with self-emptying and negation. In her published work she generally eschewed conventional life writing, and the prose style of her essays, as I've intimated, is characterised by a detached urbanity. If Sontag's initial statements of her aesthetic and her immersion in the society of the spectacle align her with postmodernism and postmodernity, her prose style connects Sontag to the impersonality of high modernism.

On one level, the conflict between Sontag's stance of impersonality and her celebrity profile is quite characteristic of literary modernism. Loren Glass notes the striking contrast between the 'theories of self-effacement' promulgated by the primary spokespeople for modernism and 'their actual practice and literary-historical destiny of self-aggrandizement and even shameless self-promotion'—exemplified, for instance, in the transformation of T.S. Eliot, propagandist for poetry as an 'escape from personality', into 'the object of an international personality cult, eventually appearing on the cover of *Time*' (5).

But while the modernists attempted to maintain a distance between their projects and the hubbub of popular culture (even if they sometimes incorporated elements of that hubbub into their own work in the service of ironic critique), Sontag, articulating 'the new sensibility', openly embraced commercialised entertainment.

Of the essays collected in *Against Interpretation*, it was 'Notes on Camp' that had the most impact. The essay—in which Sontag variously defines camp as mode of appreciation, a variety of cultural artefact, and a perception of 'the theatricalization of experience' (287)—was first published in the fall 1964 issue of *Partisan Review*, which had a circulation of less than 10,000, but it went on to have a life in less rarefied media outlets. In December of 1964, *Time* published a summary of the essay, thereby precipitating the mainstreaming of camp, a phenomenon perhaps most famously exemplified by the self-conscious ironies of the *Batman* TV series that began in 1966. *Batman* was an example of what Sontag in her essay called 'deliberate Camp...Camp which knows itself to be camp', and which she declared generally less satisfying than 'pure' or 'naïve' camp (282). In a famous formulation, Sontag proposes that the essence of pure or naïve camp is a 'failed seriousness' that elicits laughter or delight from its knowing audience (287). That audience, Sontag notes, is 'by and large' homosexual (290). Indeed, she states that camp is 'a private code, a badge of identification even, among small urban cliques' (275): a coded rendition of codification that indicates the role of camp as a mode of solidarity in pre-liberation metropolitan gay culture. The association with gay culture is compounded by the essay's designation of Oscar Wilde as its dedicatee and tutelary spirit: Wilde's epigrams provide the framework for the essay which, as the title promises, comprises a series of 'notes' rather than a carefully elaborated argument.

In one of the most controversial moments from this essay, Sontag declares: 'I am strongly drawn to Camp, and almost as strongly offended by it. That is why I want to talk about it, and why I can. [...] To name a sensibility, to draw its contours and to recount its history, requires a deep sympathy modified by revulsion' (276). The overkill of that modifying 'revulsion' has been taken by hostile gay readers of 'Notes on Camp' to indicate the 'phobic de-homosexualization of camp' that the essay as a whole performs (Miller, 'Sontag's Urbanity' 213). More reasonably, Mark Greif proposes that Sontag's distancing herself from camp was perhaps 'a fair caution to take...considering the social penalties that might be incurred by an unknown defender of homosexual "sensibility" who became too explicit'; he notes that in 1964 Sontag was afraid that the wrong disclosures about her personal life could lose her custody of her son. Yet at the time, Sontag's promotion of camp taste was also daring, even courageous. *Time* noted that 'Miss Sontag was not one to deny' the homosexual implications of camp (qtd. in Rollyson and Paddock 86).

Setting out the motivation for her essay in personal terms, as Sontag does in 'Notes on Camp', with the introduction of the speaking 'I' who is both drawn to and offended by camp, is for her an unusual and, it seems now, telling move. The distancing from gay men is real but so is the identification. If Sontag's impersonality is, on her own account, always tinctured by the personal, this uneasy association with gay men can be, and has been, read as a gesture towards, as much as it is an effacement of her own 'unconventional sexual feelings'. Terry Castle, for instance, claims that 'viewed in hindsight', 'Notes on Camp' forms part of, 'a coy yet now-unmissable "coming out"' (29). The perspective of hindsight is crucial, though; many of Sontag's gay critics, in the days before her lesbianism became common knowledge, did 'miss' this aspect of the essay. If Sontag comes out here, she indeed does so 'coyly'. On one level, a coy coming out seems oxymoronic; but Castle's formulation also gets at the intertwined dynamics of disclosure and repression that define homosexuality in modernity and postmodernity. 'Notes on Camp', that is, can be understood as operating according to the logics of the open secret and the closet, which queer critics, led by D. A. Miller and Eve Kosofsky Sedgwick, have argued are indispensable conceptual tools for understanding the reticulation of power and knowledge around queer identity from the late nineteenth century on.

In an analysis of Wilde's novel *The Picture of Dorian Gray,* Sedgwick distinguishes, yet also points to the overlap, between the 'open secret' of homosexuality and the 'empty secret' of 'male high modernism' that 'delineates . . . a split between content or thematics on the one hand and structure on the other that is stressed in favor of structure and at the expense of thematics' (165). An examination of male high modernism through the lens of antihomophobic critique, according to Sedgwick, suggests that the figuration that has had to be abjected is the figuration of 'the desired male body' (167). The modernism of such writers as Henry James, Ernest Hemingway, and Wallace Stevens is therefore a homophobic practice that bears traces of a repressed homoeroticism. The argument has not been uncontroversial. But it is, I think, suggestive for an account of Sontag's entangled relations to modernism and to homosexuality.

Sontag, as a good modernist, also champions 'structure over thematics'. Yet she does so in *Against Interpretation* as a means of promoting what has come to be known as postmodernism, in which, as she puts it, 'many established distinctions between form and content, the frivolous and the serious, and "high" and "low culture" are dismantled' (297). Sontag's challenge to the moribund devotion to high culture takes the form of an appeal to the sensuous rather than the cerebral properties of art. Because, she writes:

> the new sensibility . . . is more open to the pleasures of form and style, it is also less snobbish, less moralistic—in that it does not demand that pleasure in art necessarily be associated with edification. If art is understood as a form of discipline of the feelings and a programming of sensations, then the feeling (or the sensation) given off by a Rauschenberg painting might be like that of a song by the Supremes. (303)

In pitching the case for her aestheticism by invoking sensuous enjoyment, Sontag recalls Wilde, as well as another crypto-gay theorist, Wilde's teacher Walter Pater. In the preface to *Studies in the History of the Renaissance* (1873) Pater declares that 'the aesthetic critic regards all objects with which he has to do . . . as powers or forces, producing pleasurable sensations, each of a more or less peculiar and unique kind' (xxx). But while Wilde and Pater made cautious and indirect connections between the sensuous qualities of art and the erotic, in the statement that closes *Against Intepretation*'s title essay—'In place of a hermeneutics we need an erotics of art' (14)—Sontag fully collapses the sensuous with the sexual. Through her implicit and explicit identifications with dead gay male aesthetes and contemporary gay male culture, and through her twisting of the formalist poetics of modernism into an endorsement of the postmodern, Sontag embeds queerness in seemingly sober and impersonal prose.

In an interview from 1984, Sontag speaks of her desire 'to come out of the closet of the third person and speak in a more direct way', a desire which, she says, was driving her away from the essay form and back to fiction (*Conversations* 208). The figure strikingly captures not only the way in which the essays functioned as a kind of closet but also the way in which the closet enables the articulation of identity, even as it apparently secretes it. In the closeted expression of the essays, the first person indirectly emerges in the very act of its repression. And that first person is not simply a composite of aesthetic and intellectual perceptions, but to a pervasive and perhaps surprising extent sexualised. Mark Greif notes that 'an odd, partly disowned, seemingly extraneous but electrifying language of sex serpentines through...many of [Sontag's] essays.' Sontag cast such a powerful sexual aura not only because of her much-photographed good looks, or the interest in sexually radical texts and topics that characterised her 1960s work, but also because of the language of her essays, even if that language was 'partly disowned'.

On one level, Sontag's journals also act as a mode of closeted expression—a place in which the 'truth' of sexual identity is secretly articulated. But the first person is here unfettered and the language much franker. In 1948, the 15-year-old Sontag notes, 'I feel that I have lesbian tendencies (how reluctantly I write this).' Though her reluctance to put her lesbianism down on paper indicates the shame that unsurprisingly accompanied such a realisation in the late 1940s, her reflections on her sexuality are from the start shot through with defiance. In the same entry, she writes, 'I am very young, and perhaps the disturbing aspect of my sexual ambitions will be outgrown—*frankly I don't care*' (*Reborn* 11). Sontag did not wait long to act on her 'sexual ambitions': as a 16-year-old already attending Berkeley, Sontag was introduced to the delights and discomfitures of San Francisco gay and lesbian nightlife by her lover Harriet Sohmers. The certainty of Sontag's orientation seems to have wavered with her marriage at the age of 17 to Rieff, though the precise motivations on her part are mysterious: the journals give no clue, breaking off at the time of the marriage and resuming two years later when Sontag was chafing to free herself from it.

In a 1957 entry, Sontag describes reading 'a curt, unfair, uncharitable assessement' of herself in Sohmers' journal (*Reborn* 165). Sontag asks herself, 'Do I feel guilty about reading what was not intended for my eyes?,' answering: 'No. One of the main (social) functions of a journal or diary is precisely to be read furtively by other people (like parents + lovers) about whom one has been cruelly honest only in the journal' (165). Sontag's argument that the private journal always half-consciously solicits a reading public of one's intimates anticipates D. A. Miller's argument about the modern regime of the open secret. Drawing on Foucault's analysis of the disciplinary society, Miller argues that the private subject is produced by a carceral 'social totality'. The paradoxical phenomenon of the open secret 'registers the subject's accommodation to a totalizing system that has obliterated the difference he would make' (*The Novel and the Police* 207). On this reading, sexual identity—supposedly the most private substratum of the self—is public through and through, produced by and always implicated in the social world from which it is fondly imagined to provide a refuge. Although it is perhaps ultimately more useful to think of interiority and sociality as necessarily bound up with one another rather than isomorphic, Miller's argument—and Sontag's reflections—draw our attention to the incestuous relations of public and private utterances.

While it betrays the rhetorical efficacy of both journals and essays to suggest that they are talking about the same things in the same way, the journals enhance our understanding of the extent to which Sontag's 'sexual ambitions' were connected to her intellectual ambitions. In one passage from 1959, she writes, 'The orgasm focuses. I lust to write. The coming of orgasm is not the salvation but, more, the birth of my ego. I cannot write until I find my ego. The only kind of writer [I] could be is the kind who exposes himself' (218). Then, in another entry from a few days later: 'My desire to write is connected with my homosexuality. I need the identity as a weapon, to match the weapon that society has against me . . . Being queer makes me feel more vulnerable. It increases my wish to hide, to be invisible—which I've always felt anyway' (221). For Sontag, queer sexuality lies at the heart of contradictory desires to expose oneself and to hide within writing. These contradictory desires were to be played out in a career as a celebrity writer who barred talk of her queerness and in an impersonal writing which encoded the deeply personal fact of that queerness. But in *Against Interpretation*, that encoded admission was not simply evidence of the way in which, as Foucault argues about the post-Enlightenment regime of sexuality, 'the obligation to conceal [sex] [is] but another aspect of the duty to admit to it' (*Reborn* 61). Queerness was also used in Sontag's writing, as she says, as a 'weapon'—a subtle and subversive weapon, but a weapon nonetheless—a weapon against the orthodoxies of mid-century American intellectual life.

3

There is a sense, however, in which Sontag's rebellious impulse in *Against Interpretation* outran her. One motivation of 'Notes on Camp' is the attempt to validate an 'aristocratic' imperative of taste-making. As Sontag stresses, some-what in tension with her rejection of the 'snobbish' tendencies of 'the old sensibility', 'the history of Camp taste is part of the history of snob taste' (290). 'Camp,' Sontag announces, 'is the answer to the problem: how to be a dandy in the art of mass culture' (288). Rather than collecting and consuming rare objects like the nineteenth-century dandy, the modern camp aesthete 'learns to possess' common objects 'in a rare way': 'Camp...makes no distinction between the unique object and the mass-produced object. Camp taste transcends the nausea of the replica' (289). But if contemporary camp is so involved in mass culture—indeed, generated by it—then its transcendence can never be complete.

Camp entails a kind of ironising leveling—'the equivalence of all objects' (289); a tendency of camp that feeds into postmodern culture. Sontag both welcomed and felt unease about this development. Revisiting the issue of camp in a 1982 essay, Sontag sought to distinguish between pseudo-aristocratic camp and mainstreamed camp taste. Camp can be seen 'as part of the democratizing of dandy attitudes', but it 'still presupposes the older, higher standards of discrimination—in contrast to the taste incarnated by Andy Warhol, the franchiser and mass marketer of the dandyism of leveling' (*Where the Stress Falls* 80). As in 'Notes on Camp', the murky formulations—a democratisation of elite attitudes, the franchising of the dandyism of leveling—obfuscate the way in which camp is necessarily caught up in mass culture, even if it is (or was) distanced from majoritarian modes of consumption.

The tension in Sontag's theory of camp between transcendence of and immersion in mass culture can, I suggest, be related to a tension in her career between uniqueness and seriality. One of the most remarked-upon aspects of Sontag, and one which she arguably did much to promote, is her singularity. But this singularity was also shadowed by intimations of the repetition inherent in commodity culture, or, in Sontag's phrase, the nausea of the replica. In dubbing her the 'Dark Lady of American Letters', for instance, Norman Podhoretz wrote that this was a position 'originally...carved out by Mary McCarthy' (154–5). The idea is reinforced by the anecdote Sontag told, in which McCarthy, meeting her for the first time, pronounced 'Oh, you're the imitation me' (Bernstein). Sontag's celebrity status was premised on her singularity but also indicated her implication in the consumer capitalism that she increasingly professed to despise. The twentieth-century celebrity system, a concomitant of commodity culture, insists on the uniqueness of the individual—it is in David Marshall's formulation a manifestation of hyper-individuality (59)—but it is also driven by the imperatives of replacement and repetition. However, although there is a clear sense in which Sontag's career incorporates her in US celebrity culture (the photographs, the TV appearances, the articles in *Vogue*, and so on), her status as a *writer* also places her in an ironic and complicating relation to it.

As Loren Glass argues, theories of celebrity usually focus on 'corporate culture industries' such as film and TV, 'in which the individual agency behind the celebrity persona is clearly vitiated, if not irrelevant' (3); such theories cannot account for the status of modernist writer-celebrities, who sustain 'an ethos of individual creative production over and against the rise of [the] culture industries in which they nevertheless have...to participate' (4). As with other modernist celebrities, 'individual authorial consciousness' is central to Sontag's career, and this distinguishes her persona from that of the stars of the culture industries, in which "'celebrity" [is] the product of an impersonal system that responds to the needs of an equally vast and amorphous audience' (Glass, 4).

Sontag's simultaneous embodiment and denunciation of celebrity speaks to conflicting desires to proclaim her individuality—and to claim the fame that was the due of that individuality—and to transcend it. Celebrity was the available system through which fame could be achieved, and Sontag was hardly alone among modernist writers in either ambivalently exploiting this system, or ambivalently letting herself be exploited by it. However, Sontag resisted the acknowledgement of queer sexual identity that the celebrity system, with its interest in the public figure's private life, increasingly sought to exact. In this, she sought to best a system that, with regard to the articulation of sexual identity at least, could be said to have bested her.

In what might be seen as a last-ditch effort at this besting, when Sontag did acknowledge her queerness in the 2000 New Yorker interview, it was half-heartedly, and certainly not in relation to the term 'lesbian', or indeeed the term 'queer', terms which she had applied to herself many years earlier in her journals. I don't mean to accuse Sontag of bad faith in eschewing self-identification as a lesbian, even once it became relatively 'safe' to do so, as that self-identification may of course have changed in the years after she privately claimed it in her journals. Indeed, rather than instancing bad faith, Sontag's resistance to being publicly located under the label 'lesbian', perhaps indicates not only the tropism towards impersonality that marked her work but also the desire to stave off the nausea of the replica—the association with commodity culture that was increasingly associated with gay and lesbian subcultural identity from the late 1960s on. One outcome of the association of queerness and postmodernity was the conception of gay and lesbian lives as 'life styles'—modes of consumption—and Sontag was at pains to emphasise that in her view 'there is something deeply wrong if you speak of your life as your life style' as 'it...tend[s] to destroy a certain kind of spiritual possibility' (Conversations 171). Yet the associations with queerness and commodity culture were there from the start of her career and they continued to trouble it. The revulsion and nausea that Sontag in 'Notes on Camp' professed in the face of the commodity and queerness were offset by, and entangled with, the way she was inescapably 'drawn' to both.

Note

[1]   This formulation is Clara Tuite's paraphrase of a point made by Graeme Turner in a public lecture, 'Why Bother With Celebrity? Understanding the Production and Consumption of the Public Figure,' delivered in Melbourne in 2003. See Tuite 60.

References

Bernstein, Richard. 'Susan Sontag, as Image and as Herself'. *New York Times* 26 Jan. 1989. Web. 14 Sept. 2010.

Castle, Terry. 'Some Notes on "Notes on Camp"'. *The Scandal of Susan Sontag*. Ed. Barbara Ching, and Wagner-Lawlor Ching. New York: Columbia UP, 2009: 21–31.

Dollimore, Jonathan. *Sexual Dissidence: Augustine to Wilde, Freud to Foucault*. Oxford: Oxford UP, 1991.

Foucault, Michel. *The History of Sexuality*. Vol. 1, *An Introduction*. Trans. Robert Hurley. Harmondsworth: Penguin, 1990.

Glass, Loren. *Authors Inc.: Literary Celebrity in the Modern United States, 1880–1980*. New York: New York UP, 2004.

Greif, Mark. 'Still Superior'. *London Review of Books* 12 Feb. 2009. Web. 7 Sept. 2010.

Jameson, Fredric. *Postmodernism, or, the Cultural Logic of Late Capitalism*. London: Verso, 1991.

Marshall, P. David. *Celebrity and Power: Fame in Contemporary Culture*. Minneapolis: U of Minnesota P, 1997.

Miller, D. A. *The Novel and the Police*. Berkeley: U of California P, 1988.

———. 'Sontag's Urbanity'. *The Lesbian and Gay Studies Reader*. Ed. Henry Abelove, Michèle Aina Barale, and David M. Halperin. New York: Routledge. 212–19.

Pater, Walter. *The Renaissance: Studies in Art and Poetry*. Ed. Adam Phillips. Oxford: Oxford UP, 1986.

Podhoretz, Norman. *Making It*. New York: Random House, 1967.

Rollyson, Carl, and Lisa, Paddock. *Susan Sontag: The Making of an Icon*. New York: Norton, 2000.

Sedgwick, Eve Kosofsky. *Epistemology of the Closet*. Berkeley: U of California P, 1990.

Seligman, Craig. *Sontag and Kael: Opposites Attract Me*. New York: Counterpoint, 2004.

Sontag, Susan. *Against Interpretation*. New York: Farrar Straus Giroux, 1966.

———. *Conversations with Susan Sontag*. Ed. Leland Poague. Jackson: UP of Mississippi, 1995.

———. *Reborn: Journals and Notebooks, 1947–1963*. Ed. David Rieff. New York: Farrar Straus Giroux, 2008.

———. *Under the Sign of Saturn*. New York: Farrar Straus Giroux, 1980.

———. *Where the Stress Falls*. London: Vintage 2003.

Tuite, Clara. 'Tainted Love and Romantic Literary Celebrity'. *ELH* 74 (2007): 59–88.

How to Avoid Life Writing: Lessons from David Lynch

Nicola Evans

For several years acclaimed director David Lynch phoned in regular weather reports to a community radio station in Los Angeles. The act pokes fun at an industry in which autobiographical exploitation of star directors and name-brand authors has become a key marketing strategy in the sale of creative work. The weather is, of course, no different with David Lynch's name appended, even if Los Angeles were not famous for its unvarying sunshine. But the act also emblematises Lynch's creative use of banality as part of a consistent strategy of life withholding. This essay addresses forms of anti-life writing emerging in reaction to the current multimedia boom in confessional literature, a boom in part fuelled by the exponential growth of ancillary texts such as production diaries, commentaries and making of documentaries that purport to take us behind the scenes of a text to the lives of the people who created it. Focusing on Lynch's aptly named film *Inland Empire* and on the wealth of satellite texts that surround his films, I argue that Lynch's deployment of banality is not merely a form of mystification, but a challenge to rethink the kinds of stories that life writing genres prioritise.

In an essay examining the ethics of life writing, Paul John Eakin suggests that life writing is fundamentally an assertion of personhood: 'When we tell or write about our own lives . . . we establish ourselves as persons: I am someone, someone who has lived a valuable life, a value affirmed precisely by any life story's implicit claim that it is worth telling and hearing' (5). In the course of his essay, however, Eakin gives us reason to question whether all life stories can equally make this claim. Much of the essay focuses on the writing of exceptional lives— lives marked by suffering or oppression, narrated by people for whom the act of writing is a way of correcting a social injustice. Although Eakin, like other theorists of this genre, perceives life writing to be a formal version of something everyone does 'piecemeal every day' (5) his essay reserves praise for those life stories that are uncommon, stories that rise above 'dominant frames of interpretation' (13). Eakin's example of a life story that failed to transcend such dominant frameworks is revealing. Jonathan Franzen wrote an essay for the *New Yorker* about his experiences on the talk show *Oprah* and the attempts by the talk show producers to fit his life into a clichéd format. Franzen tries to set the record straight in the *New Yorker* by offering us a more authentic account of his life, but Eakin argues that this story is as conventional as the one that Oprah wanted, falling back disappointingly on a scenario that Eakin describes as a 'standard feature of autobiographical narrative' (14). For Eakin, the simple act of telling a life is not quite enough. In order to count, in order to confer the value of personhood, the life story must be original, a notion that presupposes individuals who somehow escape the systems—and narratives—into which they are born.

Must our life stories be told at all? If Eakin regards life writing as an act that affirms personhood, David Miller makes almost the opposite claim. Discussing the preface that Charles Dickens wrote for his fictional autobiography, *David Copperfield*, Miller points to the adroit way in which Dickens performs what we might call 'life withholding'. In his preface, Dickens tells the reader that he is having trouble leaving this book behind: 'my interest in it is so recent and strong...that I am in danger of wearying the reader I love with personal confidences and private emotions' (qtd. in Miller 196). Right on the verge of disclosing something private—something personal—Dickens stops, directing the reader instead towards his novel, *David Copperfield*. This is, as Miller observes, a good substitute, because as the title page indicates it comprises the '*personal history, adventures, experience and observation of David Copperfield...that he never meant to be published on any account*' (qtd. in Miller 196, emphasis added). Describing this move, Miller emphasises how often this pattern is found within the novel, where David, the narrator, repeatedly gestures towards intimate revelations, powerful feelings—which he nonetheless finds 'utterly beyond my power to tell'. It is not hard, as Miller points out, to guess at the secret feelings that David cannot bring himself to tell because the context often suggests what they might be. So why keep secrets? Or more precisely why does David—and Dickens—keep telling us they have a secret? Surely the best way to keep a secret is not to tell anyone that you have it.

According to Miller, the reason that both Dickens and his fictional narrator David insist on a secret self is that the possession of a private, personal terrain hung around with no entry signs is an essential criterion of the liberal subject: 'Secrecy would seem to be a mode whose ultimate meaning lies in the subject's formal insistence that he is radically inaccessible to the culture that would otherwise entirely determine him' (195). To enjoy this sense that we are free because we can keep part of ourselves secret from society, the Victorian novel offers us the pleasure of being able to penetrate the characters' secrets whilst keeping our own, the sense that 'however much [the reader] sees, he is never seen in turn' (208). Whereas Eakin perceives the telling of a life story to be a sign of a fundamental freedom, Miller, former student of Foucault, sees in life writing a dangerous yielding of the self to society by a subject willing, even eager, to confess all. Ultimately, for Miller, writing a life is a contradictory proposition, because 'the self is most itself at the moment when its defining inwardness is most secret, most withheld from writing—with the equally paradoxical consequence that autobiography is most successful only where it has been abandoned for the Novel' (200).

My goal here is not to undermine the value of life writing but to suggest that the genres of life writing might be usefully extended to include forms of anti-life writing, strategies of life withholding emerging in the wake of the boom in forms of confessional narrative proliferating across media. A good place to study tactics of life withholding is in the performance of the famously cryptic film director David Lynch. Like Dickens, Lynch is a master of deflecting the gaze of the consumer elsewhere. What interests me in Lynch is the creative use he makes of banality, a manoeuvre that invites a reassessment of the value of life stories that Eakin found problematic, those that fail to lift themselves out of the domain of the commonplace. Lynch's recent film *Inland Empire* dramatises the reasons why we should listen to stories that are all too familiar. Taking a cue from Miller, my analysis focuses not just on Lynch's film but also on cinema's version of the literary preface—the interviews, the press conferences and DVD featurettes where the life of an auteur unfolds and where Lynch, conversely, gives lessons on the tactics of life withholding.

Before discussing Lynch, I begin by tracing some parallels between authors and film auteurs. Although the director of a film differs in many respects from a literary author, what they have in common is a media marketplace in which the life of an author or an auteur plays a visible and expanding role in the distribution and reception of texts.

Authors and Auteurs

The idea that films have something like a single author and that this person should be the director was the invention of a group of French film critics in the late 1940s and 1950s writing for the journal *Cahiers du Cinema*. Seeking to raise the cultural status of film to an art form, the *Cahiers* critics borrowed heavily from literary models to reinvent the director as an artist, an 'auteur'. Proponents of auteur criticism argued that although Hollywood films were the collective product of a studio system, certain individuals such as Alfred Hitchcock, Orson Welles or Howard Hawks were capable of transcending the studio system to mark their films with the imprint of their own personal visions. It is perhaps no coincidence that many of the advocates of auteur criticism, such as Francois Truffaut, Claude Chabrol and Jean-Luc Godard—would go on to become directors themselves in the French New Wave of the 1960s. Although modelled on literary authors, the film auteur was from the beginning under different pressures. Extracted not without controversy from the large collection of people with claims to be behind the film—including the screenplay writer—the film auteur was much more obviously a fragile and imaginary construct. He couldn't hide away as easily; the whole point was to establish his existence—the film auteur needed, in other words, to be found. The idea of the auteur generated an industry of auteur criticism performing a forensic investigation of the film to find the fingerprints of this unique individual lurking in the mise-en-scene, or thematic, preoccupations of the film.

When structuralism swept through film studies in the 1960s it pushed the auteur off his perch. If not quite dead, like the literary author, the role of the film auteur in the proliferation of meaning was radically downsized. As structuralism gave way to psychoanalytic and ideological approaches to film, auteurism came to seem like a retrograde attachment to illusions of individual autonomy. Decades later, however, auteur criticism is back. The return of the auteur in film theory stems partly from recognition of the importance of auteurs as an industrial category used to market films to audiences. The strategy is not a new one. As David Bordwell observes, auteurs were a critical factor in the commercial rise of international art cinema (46). The ability to talk about a 'Bergman film' or a 'Fellini masterpiece' helped producers of art house films to draw on existing audiences for modern art, coaxing them into the cinema by speaking a familiar language of individual genius (Corrigan 102). In the case of difficult works, it was also a relief to have the personal life of the director to fall back on in attempting to make sense of the film.

Today auteurism dominates mainstream cinema too. Name-brand directors—Tarantino, Scorsese, Campion—help to identify a film for potential viewers. Corrigan introduces the idea of the 'auteur star', the auteur as a commercial performer whose life at times eclipses the film text (107). One can draw a parallel with the rising significance of the author in book publicity. Whereas the life of the author has always been important in autobiographies due to the peculiar terms of the 'autobiographical pact' that such writers make with their readers, analysts of the publishing industry suggest that the author's life story is becoming key to book sales in any genre. Kate Douglas points to evidence of the increasing demand for author tours and the multiplication of venues for author appearances, from talk shows to websites to writer's festivals. 'In today's commerce,' as Corrigan sums up, 'we want to know what our authors and auteurs look like or how they act; it is the text that may now be dead' (106).

David Lynch and the Film Preface

> Prologue means what goes before, right? That's exactly what it is. It's very important what goes on there. And no one has ever really written about that front part. (David Lynch in response to a question about the opening of *Eraserhead*, qtd. in Rodley 63)

If interest in authors and auteurs is increasing, so are the places we can look to find such information. A host of extra-textual materials accompany the release of films and books like an expanding entourage clustering around a star. Driven by the multiplication of distribution channels and the hunger for more and more content, both books and films come with a generous collection of promotional, behind-the-scenes information. In an age of media convergence, books have trailers and film auteurs have their own versions of the literary preface in the form of making of documentaries, video diaries and backstage featurettes that anticipate a film's release in the cinema and follow that film onto the DVD where they become part of the commercially valuable 'special features'. It is in these satellite spaces that the life of authors and auteurs is constructed for public consumption. But the peculiar status of these satellite texts makes them equally appropriate to a tactics of life withholding.

The peculiarity of the satellite text was foregrounded by Derrida in his essay about the literary preface. Derrida calls the preface both essential and ludicrous (9). It is essential because it sums up what the author intended to communicate in the book. It is ludicrous because if the meaning of a book could really be summed up in the preface, it could be dispensed. As glossed by Derrida's translator, prefaces exist in a 'strange warp of both time and space' (xxxii), anticipating a text that hasn't yet appeared, delaying its presence with a comment that will only make sense after it has been read. Moreover, prefaces are written, 'in view of their own self effacement (Derrida 9): '[u]pon reaching the end of the pre-... the route which has been covered must cancel itself out ...' (9). So, why write them in the first place? One answer is that the preface is often a place for autobiographical admissions where the author often reflects on the relationship of life to work. These extra-textual reflections become especially important in the case of directors such as David Lynch, whose work is notoriously baffling, a fact that puts pressure on the life of the director to yield solutions and makes the satellite texts doubly interesting.

What makes Lynch difficult in part is the way his work flouts conventional categories. He has directed critically acclaimed art house works such as *Blue Velvet* and *Wild at Heart*, which won the Palme d'Or at the Cannes Film Festival, and experimental works such as *Eraserhead*. Yet Lynch's work also includes commercial and mainstream ventures, including the science fiction adaptation *Dune*, the teaser trailer for Michael Jackson's *Dangerous* tour and the sentimental story of two brothers in *The Straight Story*, distributed by Disney. His work crosses media formats travelling from painting to film to television and comic strips and skilfully deploys the language of secrecy to tempt viewers to accompany him. In 1990–1991 David Lynch's television series *Twin Peaks* became a worldwide phenomenon in which the mystery of the murder of Laura Palmer sent viewers off on an endless scavenger hunt for clues pursued through ancillary media texts such as the publication of Laura Palmer's secret diary (written by Lynch's daughter, Jennifer) and the recordings of Dale Cooper, the key FBI detective investigating Laura's death. Such a strategic use of secrets cleverly made the substance of the UK marketing campaign for *Mulholland Drive*, in which trailers and movie posters pretended to offer the audience clues for interpreting the film provided by the director, including invitations to 'Notice the appearances of the red lampshade' and 'Notice the robe, the ashtray and the coffee cup'.

The secrets of his narratives and the difficulty of fitting his work neatly into traditional categories, generate an increased appetite for the performances of David Lynch as an auteur. The interviews, the DVD extras, the making of documentaries become texts eagerly sought out by the viewer in the hopes that Lynch will offer answers to the mysteries of his work. For a director with a reputation for revealing little, one is struck by the sheer volume of talk that David Lynch has put on record. In addition to interviews about individual films, Lynch is the subject of one full-length book of interviews now in its second edition (Rodley), two documentaries about his working process (*'Lynch (One)'* and *'Lynch 2'*), and of the many academic books devoted to his work, at least one is based on interviews with the director over several years (Nochimson, *Passion of David Lynch*). The tenor of interviews and press conferences with David Lynch may be summed up by the first speaker at the Cannes press conference following the screening of *Mulholland Drive*: 'Mr Lynch, please explain.' It is a request that Lynch invariably frustrates, but it is his way of refusing that interests me here, a refusal that begins to make sense of how a director who talks so much can preserve a reputation for telling us nothing.

Consider, for example, a characteristic exchange between *Guardian* journalist Mark Kermode and David Lynch during an interview held at the National Film Theatre in London in front of a packed audience in 2007. The interview was included on a disc of 'bonus features' accompanying the DVD release of *Inland Empire*. Observing a recurrence of images of electricity in Lynch's films, Kermode attempted a complicated explanation of what electricity might symbolise. As his explanation wound down, Kermode said:

> MK: I know you hate saying what things mean in your films, but am I right in thinking that that's at least in the right area?

> DL: No...(audience laughs and some applaud)...Mark you're a...what a beautiful guy Mark is...I didn't think about that. I just like electricity.

Or consider the hapless French journalist in an interview included in the DVD extras for *Mulholland Drive*, who asks Lynch, 'Did you want to recreate a special world like in *Twin Peaks*, for example?' To which Lynch responds: 'Every film is a world. You go into a theatre, it becomes dark and you enter a new world. Wonderful things happen in these worlds. And it's the magic of cinema.'

As such answers demonstrate, Lynch's replies to questions are not enigmatic or jargon ridden—he speaks plainly and precisely, and if not answering the implied question, he always answers the literal one. But sooner or later every interviewer runs into the cul-de-sac of Lynch's implacable banality. He speaks a language that is simple and often childlike, referring to the painter Francis Bacon as 'the main guy, the number one kinda hero painter' (Lynch 16) and frequently using boyish exaggerations: 'that just *kills* me' or 'it's so *weird*'. When asked about his creative process, his answers are stunning in their recourse to the obvious: 'you try to get the right person for the role' he told a journalist at the aforementioned Cannes press conference for Mulholland Drive when asked about his casting choices.

The way in which Lynch meets the curious with an escalating display of ordinariness—the four-word biography that he once provided for the *Wild At Heart* press kit was 'Eagle Scout, Missoula Montana' (Rodley 5) has become a well-established part of his persona. Described as a 'Jimmy Stewart from Mars' by one of his producers, interviewers often contrast the ordinary sweetness of his demeanour outside his films (Jimmy Stewart) with the horrors and absurdities inside his films (Mars) and by extension, Lynch's unconscious mind. Reviewers like to reference the opening scene in *Blue Velvet* in which the camera descends from the grassy lawn of a 1950s-style American suburb to uncover a seething mix of insects feeding on decay beneath the surface. Such dichotomies between normal surfaces and the unpleasantness beneath are comforting because they appear to settle exactly where what is disturbing is to be found and where safety lies. We know, in other words, where we are supposed to look; we know that the ordinary surface is what we are supposed to look away from to the more interesting secrets that it disguises. In *Lynch on Lynch*, one finds the interviewer doing his best to superimpose this hermeneutic model of reading on the life of the director, intimating a hidden set of terrors lurking in Lynch's childhood through a series of very leading questions such as 'Looking at your work, one might surmise that you were frightened by many things as a child. Were you?' (Rodley 6). Lynch's manner of replying to these questions is instructive. Compliantly, he agrees that he was frightened, although immediately suggests that his fear was no more than any child feels. The re-establishment of normalcy, however, is immediately followed by a serious discussion of his sister's fear of green peas: 'I think it was something to do with the consistency and strength of the outer surface and then what was inside when you broke that membrane . . . But I don't know you'd have to ask her' (6). In such remarks, Lynch demonstrates a constant defiance of conventional schemes for distinguishing normal from strange. Frequently, his responses mix the two together. When asked about the experience of making *Eraserhead*, Lynch responds, 'we were putting on our own play, you know what I mean? It was so fantastic. And I had my paper route! And soybeans. I was really into soybeans then' (Lynch 75). And the soybeans, it must be emphasised, get the same serious attention as his film.

The elevation of banality is exemplified in Lynch's weather reports. For a number of years Lynch telephoned a radio station in Los Angeles to report on the weather. The practice continues on his website DavidLynch.com where visitors can enjoy Lynch describing the sunshine and current temperature, and Lynch's weather report is the opening scene of the first documentary about Lynch covering the period during which Lynch made the film *Inland Empire*. At one level, the practice pokes fun at the commerce of auteurism, testing our willingness to consume something that has the Lynch brand name attached. The weather is, of course, no different when communicated by David Lynch than by anyone else. The joke is two-fold since Los Angeles is famous as a place of monotonous sunshine, where there is often little weather to report. Yet, to dismiss this as simply a joke is to accept that what is common to everyone is not worthy of our interest. The term 'banality' as Kaplan observes, is ambivalent—it can mean trivial, but it 'has as one of its meanings the sense "open to the use of the entire community", a "common (shared) place" (43). The appending of his name to information about the weather that cannot be owned by anyone is consistent with the kind of life stories that Lynch tells in his films, which for all their trappings of secrecy are nonetheless very familiar stories of both men and women in trouble. Taking the weather reports seriously for a moment means considering the possibility that the search for hidden horrors is a diversion and that Lynch's life is hiding in the light, too banal to be noticed.

The process by which Lynch redirects attention towards the commonplace is dramatised in his film *Inland Empire*, the title of which plays knowingly on two levels, at once a reference to an unconscious presumed hidden away and (as Lynch was happy to reveal in interviews), the name of an unremarkable inland metropolitan area in southwest Los Angeles. Following the title of the film, the first shot is a black and white close up of a gramophone needle travelling the grooves of a record as a static laden voice announces, 'Europe's longest running radio play continuing in the Baltic region in an old hotel'. As the recording fades, a prostitute and her client walk up the corridor of an old hotel to the room in which they will have sex. We hear the prostitute saying that she does not know where she is but we cannot fully see either person because their faces are blanked out like crime scene footage from a surveillance camera—the comparison facilitated by the fixed high angle from which the scene of the sexual encounter is shot. Nor can we entirely hear these characters since they speak in Polish, although their conversation is subtitled. The subsequent scene offers us the same woman, this time in colour, sitting in a hotel room crying as she watches a television screen covered with white static. We cut to a live stage on which three humans, their identities concealed by large rabbit costumes, exchange non sequiturs about secrets in English that are interrupted at random moments by canned laughter and two Polish men in a grand room with old-fashioned furnishings who exchange passionate remarks about their search for an opening.

The sequence as a whole displays a nested structure of multiple media forms framing different fictional worlds. It serves as a prologue to what is usually treated by reviewers of the film as the main plot, a story about a Hollywood actress named Nicky Grace who is cast in a film that is intended to be her comeback. During rehearsals of the film, Nicky Grace discovers that her comeback film is a remake of an earlier film based on an old Polish folktale, a film that was abandoned when the two leads were murdered. Gradually, Nicky Grace, the actress, and her fictional role begin to merge, as she loses sight of which is which and begins a free fall through the nested story structure, becoming by turns the working-class wife of an abusive husband, a married woman having an affair with a lying Southern gentleman called Smithy and a world-weary prostitute who delivers a monologue describing acts of violence by men, although none of the men have names: 'it doesn't matter what his name was' she says, 'it's an old story.'

The grounds for treating Grace's story as the main story of the film lie in the casting. *Inland Empire* is subtitled 'A woman in trouble', and that woman, in the eyes of reviewers, is Nicky Grace, played by Laura Dern, an actress known for her roles in Lynch films and elsewhere and who is surrounded by other recognisable 'name' actors, including Jeremy Irons, who plays the director of her comeback film, as well as Grace Zabriski, Justin Theroux and Harry Dean Stanton, all regular members of Lynch's productions. Conversely, the scenes that precede the entrance of Laura Dern are full of characters with no names—the prostitute in the hotel is simply referred to as the 'lost girl' in the credits, the Polish man arguing in the ballroom is the 'Phantom'—and when these characters are not played by unknown Polish actors, their identity is obscured by the camera (the blanked out faces) or by an enormous rabbit head. It is predictable that most reviewers should choose not to write about the 'front bit' or when they do, treat it as a method of intensifying the audience's desire for the appearance of Laura Dern (Nochimson 'Inland Empire'). But to assume that the woman in trouble of the film's subtitle is the American actress Nicky Grace is to ignore the way her story is framed by the story of the lost Polish girl which bookends the film. The prologue of *Inland Empire* occupies the same warp of time and space in which Derrida situates the preface. It precedes and foreshadows events that occur in the narrative of Nicky Grace both through a flash forward glimpsed on the television screen in the hotel room and through the lost Polish girl who is the first woman in trouble we meet. Moreover, the story of the lost Polish girl outlasts Grace's story, as the closing of the film shows us the Polish girl reunited with her husband and son. The prologue refuses to stay outside the text, working its way into the Hollywood narrative as the story of Nicky Grace is gradually taken over by Polish characters: her servant, Henry, starts out speaking English but is soon and inexplicably speaking Polish, her husband turns out to be Polish, her film is based on a Polish folktale, and so on. Like plants reclaiming a decaying building, the Polish story successively replaces the American story, old world reclaiming the territory of the new. Grace's free fall through different characters ends with her assuming the role of prostitute, wandering the halls of an old hotel and entering the bedroom of the Polish girl where she immediately disappears.

The prologue is not just both inside and outside the Hollywood story— its status with respect to the film text is equally ambiguous. The mysterious references to Europe's oldest running radio play, the close-ups of gramophones and the sound of canned laughter lead us out of the film text into other texts, as does the scene of the humanoid rabbits taken from a series of webisodes that Lynch released before *Inland Empire*. Rather than containing an original life story, *Inland Empire* offers us a banal life story, a commonplace story of women in trouble; it is, as Nicky Grace says in her role as a common prostitute, a 'very old story'. *Inland Empire* is a text fraying at the edges, spilling into other media, spreading out to tell a life story that is overly familiar and not owned by anyone in particular.

In *Lynch on Lynch*, the director memorably discussed the way names and the baggage they carry can interfere with our appreciation of the things those names describe:

I could change my name! I thought about that, because names are weird things. When you say "pus", you know, there's so many things that come along with that word. A very nice photo of a pile of pus—labelled "Pus"—could be pretty cool. (Rodley 29)

The responses by reviewers to *Inland Empire* focusing on Nicky Grace vividly illustrate the power of names and name brands to direct attention in the world. At the same time, Lynch's framing of the story in a prologue devoted to an unknown woman in trouble might be said to exhibit the same desire that his conversations about peas and soybeans exhibit in interviews—the desire to shake free of the stricture of names, including his own, and to make us look again at the compelling stories that we have in common. If *Inland Empire*, like Lynch's performance as an auteur, ultimately frustrates the quest to discover a secret, it is evidence for David Miller's claim that what is really interesting about secrets are the reasons we choose to keep them.

References

Blue Velvet. Dir. David Lynch. Perf. Isabella Rosselini, Kyle MacLachlan, Dennis Hopper. De Laurentiis Entertainment Group, 1986. Film.

Bordwell, David. 'Authorship and Narration in Art Cinema.' *Film and Authorship*. Ed. V. Wright Wexman New Jersey: Rutgers University Press, 2003.

Corrigan, Timothy. *A Cinema Without Walls: Movies and Culture after Vietnam*. New Jersey: Rutgers University Press, 1991.

Derrida, Jacques. *Dissemination*. Trans. Barbara Johnson. Chicago: University of Chicago Press, 1981.

Douglas, Kate. 'Blurbing Biographical: Authorship and Autobiography.' *Biography* 24.4 (2001): 806–26.

Eakin, Paul John. 'Mapping the Ethics of Life Writing'. *The Ethics of Life Writing*. Ithaca: Cornell University Press, 2004.

Eraserhead. Dir. David Lynch. Perf. Jack Nance, Charlotte Stewart, Allen Joseph. Libra Films International, 1977. Film.

Inland Empire. Dir. David Lynch. Perf. Laura Dern, Jeremy Irons, Justin Theroux. Optimum, 2007. DVD. Special Edition.

Lynch, David. *Lynch on Lynch*. Rev. ed. Ed. Chris Rodley. New York: Faber and Faber, 2005.

Lynch (one). Dir. blackANDwhite. Absurda, 2007. DVD.

Lynch 2. Dir. blackANDwhite. Inland Empire. Dir. David Lynch. Madman Entertainment, 2007. DVD. Disc 2.

Lynch, David. "Interview with Mark Kermode." Inland Empire. Dir. David Lynch. Madman Entertainment, 2007. DVD. Disc 2.

Lynch, David. "Cannes 2001 Press Conference." Mulholland Drive. Dir. David Lynch. Optimum, 2007. DVD. Special Edition. Disc 2.

Miller, David A. *The Novel and the Police*. Berkeley: University of California Press, 1988.

Mulholland Drive. Dir. David Lynch. Perf. Naomi Watts, Laura Harring, Justin Theroux. Les Films Alain Sarde, 2001. Film.

Nochimson, Martha. *The Passion of David Lynch: Wild at Heart in Hollywood*. Austin: University of Texas, 1997.

———. 'Inland Empire'. *Film Quarterly* 60.4 (2007): 10–14.

Rodley, Chris., Lynch on Lynch. New York: Faber and Faber, 2005.

The Straight Story. Dir. David Lynch. Perf. Richard Farnsworth, Sissy Spacek. Asymmetrical
   Productions, 1999. Film.
Twin Peaks. By Mark Frost and David Lynch. Perf. Kyle MacLachlan, Michael Ontkean,
   Madchen Amick. American Broadcasting Company 1990–1991. Television series.
Wild at Heart. Dir. David Lynch. Perf. Nicholas Cage, Laura Dern, Willem Dafoe. Polygram,
   1990. Film.

The Other Side of the Curtain

Irene Lucchitti

Marta Becket was born in New York in 1924 into a life immersed in the arts. As an infant, she listened to her mother's music at home and attended the theatre with her father, theatre critic Henry Beckett. The crib in which she slept, flooded with flickering neon lights, became her first performance space as she tried within its confines to replicate what she had seen in the theatre. Throughout her childhood and in the days of her youth, she trained in ballet and in art. In her early career, she worked on Broadway, dancing in *A Tree Grows in Brooklyn* and *Wonderful Town* and working as a Radio City Music Hall Rockette. She developed a one-woman show with which she toured the country until the life-changing day in 1967 when she happened upon an abandoned theatre in Death Valley Junction. She soon made it her own and re-fashioned it as the Amargosa Opera House. In this most unlikely place, she has performed works of her own creation for more than 40 years. In its appearance, format and content, Becket's autobiography, *To Dance on Sands*, which appeared in 2007, reflects a life only truly lived in art and on stage. The dissenting voice of the author is heard on every page, as she considers and refuses anything that might compromise her life as an artist or the art itself. This paper will consider Becket's early inter-related wishes to enter ever 'other' worlds and to create an exoticised self as expressions of a personal and artistic dissent that, while seeming to find fulfilment in her self-positioning in Death Valley Junction, produces a self that is both theatricalised and elusive.

W E B Du Bois once famously described his autobiography as 'the soliloquy of an old man who dreams of what his life has been, as he sees it slowly drifting away, and what he would like others to believe' (12). His remarks, which point to the imaginative, dramatic and performative aspects of life writing, its intimate links with questions of mortality as well as to the creativity and selectivity in its design and purpose, are pertinent to an appreciation of Marta Becket's autobiography *To Dance on Sands* (2007), which charts her journey from a life within the arts community in New York City to a solitary life as a company-of-one in the badlands of Death Valley. It depicts a life of dissent that takes the form of a steadfast refusal of the mundane, of the ordinary, of the domestic and of the intimate. Her immersion in her artistic pursuits is shown repeatedly to be a performance of dissent and her various projects as refuge from the modes of life she rejects so resolutely.

Trained as a ballerina, artist, musician, composer and writer, Becket left New York to make a home in Death Valley Junction where she established the Amargosa Opera House in 1967. Although she is now in her 80s, Becket still performs regularly on her own stage in the town where she is the only permanent resident. The story she tells reflects a complex psychology and a lifelong concern with aesthetics, with the relationships between beauty and feeling, between art and life.

Although a cult figure in some circles and the subject of the documentary *Amargosa*, Becket's story is not widely known. The facts of her life are related in two pamphlets she wrote for sale in the shop of her Opera House (1998; 2003). She was born Martha Becket in New York in 1924 to parents on the verge of divorce. She lived with her mother in straitened circumstances and moved often to ever cheaper accommodation. From her earliest days, Becket was immersed in the arts with music in her home and regular visits to the theatre with her father (*Before the Amargosa Opera House* 1–2). In her youth, she trained in ballet and art before dancing on Broadway (2). Although she worked diligently, her career progressed fitfully as vaudeville and the variety club circuit lost their popularity to television (4–6). Seeing her name misspelt as 'Marta Becket' on a playbill one day and, preferring it so, she remained 'Marta Becket' for the rest of her life (*To Dance on Sands* 119). She married Tom Williams in 1961 (*Before the Amargosa Opera House* 10), and styling herself 'a company of one', toured the country with him, presenting a one-woman show until the day they happened upon the abandoned theatre in Death Valley Junction which they rented and re-fashioned as the Amargosa Opera House. She put together a programme of performances each year and, with Tom as MC, performed each of her scheduled shows in their entirety whether she had an audience or not. She also painted the inside walls of the Opera House with murals depicting a Renaissance audience and adorned the ceiling with celestial imagery (*Before the Amargosa Opera House* 21–4).

After her marriage failed, Tom Willett, affectionately known as Wilget, stepped in to assist Becket in the running of the Opera House. He also shared the stage with her, emceeing her performance and complementing it with his own comic antics (*Before the Amargosa Opera House* 24–5). They worked together and were close companions for 17 years, sharing meals and television, but living separately until his sudden death. He is the only person she ever refers to as her partner, the only person from whom she does not dissent (*To Dance on Sands* 324–5). Becket feels the full impact of her life choices most keenly after his death, when being 'a company of one', or a 'one-woman show', is no longer a boast but a sad and lonely reality (327). His death, as she writes it, leaves her feeling loss and lack—even on stage—for the first time in her life. She offers a theatrical rendition of his absence by continuing to perform the shows designed for two, leaving gaps in the spaces Wilget had filled (327). She paints him into a circus backdrop to her show, depicting him as a lion tamer and a strong man and makes a clown doll called Wilget with which to dance (328).

The paratext in which Becket's book is encased, that part of the book in which author, publisher and reader meet (Genette xvii), is elaborate and densely packed with significances that bleed into the text itself. As a physical object, Becket's book reflects many aspects of Du Bois' description of life writing. It offers many clear signs of the 'life' the elderly Becket wants us 'to believe' as it signals the theatrical nature of the autobiographical persona we will encounter within its covers. The title *To Dance on Sands*, a phrase drawn from *Two Gentlemen of Verona*, draws attention to Becket's anomalous juxtaposition of the high arts of theatre and ballet, usually associated with great metropolitan centres and the shifting sands of the desert, while the sub-title, *The Life and Art of Death Valley's Marta Becket*, signals the inseparability of life and art in Becket's story. It also indicates that the exotic location in which Becket has lived is an intrinsic part of her self-fashioning.

The photographic images that dominate the cover of the book—a highly stylised photograph of Becket as a young ballerina superimposed over a sepia-toned photograph of the Amargosa Opera House—hint at a concern with the questions of mortality that preoccupied Du Bois and bear out Roland Barthes' view that death is intrinsic to the images produced by photography (14–5). They also offer several layers of significance, the *studium* and *punctum* of Barthes' theory. While the *studium* of the image of the youthful ballerina as a colourful presence in a dun landscape offers a declaration of the autobiographical persona Becket wishes to project—in Barthes' terms, 'the one' she thinks she is as well as 'the one' she wants others to think she is (13)—there is also something undeniably mournful, a *punctum*, in the photograph of a youth long past combined with the sepia tones of the old building. The old-fashioned, artificial pinkness of the ballerina draws attention to the passing of time, reminding us that this ballerina is now a frail, elderly woman. The composition of the photograph offers a poignant image of Marta Becket's Death Valley as a place where human aspiration and desolation are never too far apart and, with its portrait of artistic grace and fading light, a suggestion of her forlorn hope that art might survive the passing of time. At a late point in the text, Becket muses: 'I thought by becoming a dancer, I could become like Peter Pan, always in flight, forever dancing, forever striving for beauty. I didn't realise how short-lived a dancer's life is. Unfortunately, being a dancer does not make us immortal'(217).

The paratext further supports Becket's identification as artist with an anonymous commentary on the flap of the front cover and on the first two (un-numbered) pages of the book. These sections of the paratext, designed to be read before the text itself, predispose the reader to subscribe to the mythologising of Becket's life, presenting her as an artist responding to her own muses and the Amargosa Opera House as a mythic space. In an article in the *Guardian*, Oliver Berry of *The UK Guardian* writes that: 'The old hall that became an opera house arises mirage-like from the sands at a lonely cross-roads in Death Valley'. Todd Robinson describes it as 'the most desolate place in America' and as a place that 'offers the chance to live life on your own terms'. The anonymous commentator describes it as 'a remote ghost town a world removed from the glitz of Becket's native New York' and 'a place of artistic rebirth'. Her decision to live and perform in this unlikely place is seen to speak to Becket's character. She is 'the real thing', according to the *Northern California Bohemian*, and, to the anonymous commentator, 'fiercely independent woman driven by her creative muses to live life very much on her own terms'. For another, Becket represents 'the spirit of the individual, the spirit of the theatre, the spirit of creativity'. The anonymous commentary ends with the assertion that Becket's story will 'inspire the dancer and artist inside everyone'.

It is unlikely that Becket's artistic career would have drawn such attention had she remained in New York. Death Valley, which has long held sway over the American imagination, is much more than the setting of Becket's life and life writing. As it contributes significantly to the myth and aura that has grown up around her and, more significantly, is a constituent part of her self-fashioning as the grand canvas against which she has performed her life, we will digress for a moment to consider what Death Valley might represent. Becket tells of her first encounter with images of the American deserts in the Natural History Museum in New York: '"Was there such a place?" I wondered. The serenity and peace, endless space of pale colours of sand and sky seemed like a perfect canvas for dreams' (*To Dance on Sands* 40).

Becket's idyll, Death Valley, is the hottest, driest place in the United States of America. With its mysterious moving stones, shifting sands and rippling dunes, its craters, castles and canyons, it offers many visions of strange, harsh beauty. It is home to a great many ghost towns, mining towns set up in haste and abandoned just as hastily when the rushes were over. Over the centuries, Shoshone Indians, Chinese miners, Basque settlers and Japanese war internees have lived there and fortune-hunters, miners, mule-teams, con-men, outlaws, hippies and the doomed heroes known as the Lost Forty-Niners have all passed through (NPS). Neither doomed nor transient, Marta Becket's name has, for more than 40 years, occupied a unique spot in this list. The Valley's place-names constitute a 'lexicon of despair' (Findley 74) and attest to the human suffering it has witnessed: Arsenic Springs, Badwater, Coffin Canyon, Dante's View, Deadman Pass, Desolation Canyon, Funeral Mountains, Furnace Creek, Hell's Gate, Starvation Canyon and Suicide Pass, among others. In contrast to these melancholy names, Becket added the proud 'Amargosa Opera House', a name that called up the past but heralded a future.

Returning to Becket's text, we see that, in keeping with its theatrical cover, the text itself is dramatic in form, with a Prologue, an Overture, Acts and Scenes rather than Chapters. Its format reflects Becket's view of life as theatre and theatre as life and is constructed to reinforce the cover's signal that this autobiography is offering a theatrical version of self. Such toying with genre also enacts a performance of the theme of dissent that permeates Becket's autobiographical narrative and characterises the autobiographical persona she presents. While the text is an autobiography and therefore promises a truth-telling of sorts (Smith and Watson pp. 12–13), Becket's formatting of her text as though it were the script for a theatrical performance disrupts the autobiographical pact with the reader (Lejeune 3). It not only colours the autobiographical persona she is creating, it also affects her relationship with her readers by keeping them at arm's length or, in Becket's own words, 'on the other side of the footlights' (206).

When Becket's autobiographical stage is thoroughly set, when her audience has been prepared for her written performance of a performing self, she uses her Overture to introduce herself, her place, her art and her broad theme of dissent. She concludes her Overture in the manner of an MC introducing a stage act, an act that is her life: 'I am very much here and very much alive. And now, almost forty years later, I am pleased to present my life'. Her readership is her new audience. This autobiography is a performance.

Throughout the text, Becket presents her life as though it were staged. Her life writing thus becomes a new performance of a performance of life. The autobiographical persona she creates is always the leading character in her own drama. She places herself centre-stage in every scene, in various communities of belonging all of which she repudiates—her family, the New York performance community, her marriage partner and the community she goes to live among in Death Valley Junction. Her relationship to the various arts she practises defines the autobiographical persona she calls into being in the pages of her book. Her unswerving devotion to her own evolving notion of art and of herself as an artist marks every page, as does her singular belief in her own artistic excellence and exceptionality. As John Mulvihill observes, 'she has created a world of her own and cast herself in the role of prima ballerina for all time' (3).

Becket's fidelity to her muse at the expense of all else is both source and symptom of her deep dissent which is built into the fabric of her written life. Dissent takes several forms in this life: as a desire for an exotic identity and as a desire for a life elsewhere. We hear her dissenting voice as she considers and refuses anything that might compromise her life as an artist or the art itself and recognise, in her self-positioning in Death Valley, the fulfilment of the personal and artistic dissent she expresses.

Becket peppers her account of her unstable childhood with its many shifts to new premises, new schools and new studios with expressions of related desires to be in another world or to build another world, desires that she finds she can fulfil in the theatre or the studio. While the successive apartments she shares with her mother, often presented almost as *mise-en-scenes*, offer a version of 'home' only when her doll and her blocks come out of the packing crates; more than once she tells us that she experiences the feeling of 'coming home' or 'being home' when she enters a performance space where she might develop her craft.

Time and time again, she presents us with 'threshold moments' when she is in one world, hoping to enter another—a new art studio perhaps, or a ballet studio, or backstage in a theatre. These spaces allow her *entrée* into worlds even further removed from her realities—the world of ballet, the world of the Turkish fairy tale or the Russian folk-tale. The importance of these threshold moments to her life and to her story might be gleaned from the fact that it was Becket's original intention to call her autobiography *The Other Side of the Curtain* (Flinchum 3).

She recounts many experiences of losing herself in these other worlds when she tells us that the 'real' world and theatre sometimes swap places in her mind. One such event occurred in her infancy when she visited the theatre with her father (3). The doorman of the theatre looks like a tin soldier to the young Marta and the production on the stage seems to be a fantasy coming to life before her eyes. Life and art seem to be inverted. She conveys very vividly the psychological slippage that occurs as she negotiates the passage from the life of the theatre and the imagination to her life in the 'real' world. As she emerges from the experience, life seems wooden while art is a living thing. On another such occasion, she conveys a sense of loss as she leaves the opera—she feels she is leaving another exquisite world, far more beautiful than the real world (5). She wants to be part of this world that she finds infinitely preferable to a real world she describes as 'transparent' (31). In later years, when performing in a ballet, she feels herself 'become' the character and enter another place and time and experiences the 'return to self' as a deep shock (63). In her efforts to have us 'believe' exclusively in the artistic character of the Marta Becket persona inscribed in the text, Becket loses or abandons her inner sense of self.

Her uneasy relationship with place finds a counterpart in her imagined relationships with inanimate objects. Her 'block people' form her first audience as she crafts her childish plays and dances (6). They accompany her through life, help her settle in to new homes and speak to her at other times of stress. Only once, when she is deeply afraid, do they fail her in time of need. The murals she paints at various stages through her life—at Sandor's dance studio and in one of the apartments she lives in—seem to 'call out' to her as she leaves them behind, voicing the distress Becket herself is experiencing in leaving a treasured place (pp. 65–66). Her doll, Echo, also speaks to her, and she sometimes pretends she is a doll herself (14). And when she peeks inside the derelict Corkhill Hall in Death Valley, she hears it speaking to her, begging her to give it life (283). Later, when she is tempted to leave, she hears it begging her to stay (328).

Becket's losing of herself in these other worlds and in these relationships is matched by her desire for an exoticised self, awakened by seeing a performance of *Sheherezade* which transports her to a world that is for her somehow foreign yet intelligible (30). Soon after, she finds herself smitten by a performance by the Ballet Russe and imagines its dancers living off-stage lives of beauty, void of ordinariness. Perhaps being Russian allowed access to the world of ballet, she thinks, and from then on she wants to be Russian. For the next few years, she takes a Russian stage-name when dancing and signs her sheet-music Olga Marnoff (34)—once again abandoning self in the very search for it.

While Becket wants us to encounter and 'believe' in the resolutely artistic identity of the self she produces and performs in her text, in her devotion to her craft and in the stability and permanence of her 40-year career in the desert, the text also offers glimpses of a somewhat ghostly Marta Becket whose elusive self is never fully realised. Her whole life, as produced and performed in this text, has been a long series of performances in which she has been a character—the lead character—playing a succession of roles.

The first of these is the infant Marta who is credited with a precocious artistic sensibility and an awareness that dance was her vocation. The crib in which this young Marta slept became her first performance space as she tried within its confines to replicate the things she had seen in the theatre. The shaft of sunlight that fell upon it by day and the flickering neon lights that flooded it by night were her first spotlights, and her set of blocks became the block people who would remain her faithful companions and audience for years. She presents us with several vignettes that demonstrate the young Marta's artistic sensitivities and inclinations. We see her standing motionless for hours beside the tree at a Christmas party, pretending to be a doll in a beautiful lavender organdie dress (14). We see her later entering Sandor's studio for the first time and seeing it as a Dégas painting come to life (57) and later still, attempting a Dégas pose herself when she is working as a model (88). The onset of puberty launches her into a role for which she was unprepared: her menstruation casts her in the role of a prisoner who is being tortured and punished (73). It is soon followed by her account of the rites of passage out of childhood and into her professional life as a performer: getting her glossies taken, her social security number and her stage-name (78–9).

As her narrative advances, Becket allows us to see her performing certain roles in relation to the people close to her as well as the impact of her dissenting attitudes towards them. So deeply dissenting was her relationship with her father that she called him 'Mana' (a man), withholding from him any paternal form of address (3). There is a certain ambivalence in his relationship with the young Marta: while it was he who exposed the child to the theatre, its magic and the possibility of an artistic life, it is not long before his sudden, unannounced reappearances cause an acute anxiety that can only be assuaged by artistic endeavour or the companionship of Marta's block people. As Becket's narrative continues, she uses their relationship to enact the tension between artist and critic. Her relationship with Mana becomes one of relentless contest: he criticises her work repeatedly and gives unwanted advice which she steadfastly ignores, all the while yearning for his approval. While he dismisses the favourable reviews she gets for her shows on tour with the mantra, 'yes, but it's not New York', she responds to his dismissive criticism with a mantra of her own: 'when you ask me to stop following my dream you are asking me to die' (154).

Her relationship with her mother is no less fraught than her relationship with her father and certainly more complex. As her story progresses, Becket expresses an increasing resentment of the mother who will not let her go, who will not let her grow up and who wants to continue sleeping by her side when she is more than 30 years old. She uses the image of a mirror several times to express the emotional toll her mother's possession of her life is taking. At the height of her distress, she looks into her dressing room mirror after a performance only to see her mother's face peering back out at her. It is a moment in which Becket's self is lost to her, her presence obscured by the image of her mother staring back at her. On a later occasion, when she is apart from her mother, she glances into her mirror again to find her own face reflected back to her for the first time, but once again, the sense of self is incomplete as it is the absence of the mother's face in the mirror that is the remarkable feature of the mirror.

In his theorising of the mirror stage of development, Jacques Lacan writes that a child's encounter with the mirror image of itself gives the child a necessary but false sense of its own coherent and autonomous identity and goes on to demonstrate that such an identity is a fictive construct (1–8). Becket's mirror narratives make clear the psychic damage done to her by a mother who prevents the separation necessary to her development of a sense of self. The fictive construct of self that Becket asserts in her text, that of the arts practitioner living in an artistic realm where all aspects of humdrum existence is denied, is destabilised by the mirror events which show Becket realising 'I am not there' and resisting the unspoken possibility that 'I am not here' in a moment of recognition of a self not realised.

We see the performative nature of Becket's sense of self most clearly in her account of her marriage to Tom Williams. Furthering her self-portrait as artist, she first explains that her consent to the marriage lies with a discussion of Tom's interest in her work. Gradually, however, it becomes clear that Becket also saw marriage to Tom as a kind and respectable way to leave her mother. She admits that even though she is not sure that she is suited to the role of a wife, she is tired of the role of the dutiful daughter. Her willingness to perform the role of wife is thus a performance of dissent from her mother's impositions.

Becket describes the familiar psychological slippage in the collision between life and art in her account of the days leading up to their wedding. She feels as though she is about to act a scene in a play, in a role for which she was unsuited (252). As she settles into marriage, she avoids acts of intimacy by painting the opera house until Tom has fallen asleep. While the tension between them grows apace with her obsession with her murals (303) and the lack of physical intimacy in their lives, her painting and dancing help her to forget that she is married and might thus be seen as a performance of dissent against sexuality and marriage.

She describes the eventual disintegration of her marriage in theatrical terms— she has failed in the role of wife. Her dissent finds its fullest expression in response to Tom's reproaches: 'I was tired of trying to be a good wife. I had been a good daughter for so long now; what I really wanted to be was a good dancer, a fine painter, a good me' (305). It is clear when they mark their 10th wedding anniversary that their marriage is all but over—'the evening went well, like a smooth performance of a play that has lost its heart'. Becket's reaction to the end of her marriage is flattened and lifeless (312).

Becket's representation of a staged life impacts necessarily upon her representation of her successive audiences. Her block people were her first and perhaps ideal audience for many years. Then, in her Opera House, she sometimes played only for the benefit of the tumbleweeds that rolled around her floor. At moments such as these, when Becket is both performer and audience, one must wonder if she can be certain as to which side of the curtain is her true domain. And when there is an audience, she pays them little heed. She has been taught not to yearn for public approval, as popularity is nothing more than a sign that you have appealed to the lowest common denominator (186). Here and there throughout her text she disparages her audience, wanting to keep them at bay and to keep their hands off her art. As she manipulates the genre of autobiography in dressing her story up as a drama, she creates a camouflage that keeps her readership at a similar distance, as well as herself from herself. Her Spanish audience painted on the walls is a logical successor to her audience of block people: it provides her art with an appropriate setting while the royal status of her painted patrons dignifies her art. And best of all, it is an audience that cannot speak or interfere with her art. Her creation of inanimate audiences at one and the same time constitutes an act of dissent and prevents any possible dissent from outside her own closed circuit.

The autobiographical persona that emerges from this written performance of Becket's life appears self-contained and self-sufficient. She is the centre of her own world, in a world of one for most of her years. Major events are mentioned in passing only as they relate to her career—her one-woman art show in New York fails because of the assassination of John Kennedy, her story in *Life* magazine is delayed by coverage of the Manson story and her father's death occurs just before the biggest weekend she would ever have at the Opera House. She has spent most of her life aloof from other people, untouchable in a world that revolves around her evolving concept of art and conception of self as an artist.

But while she states repeatedly throughout the text that her central relationship is with her self and her imagination and that she is her own best friend, it is clear that her self continues to elude her in this written performance of a staged life. The self that emerges from the text is splintered by its contrasting representations of an uneasy relationship with her body and a close relationship with her imagination. While she frequently says that her imagination is her friend and her refuge, she speaks of her body with a certain ambivalence as though it were an entity outside her self. On one hand, her deep reluctance for physical intimacy causes her to wish she could stay in her child's body forever. On the other hand, she sees her body as a valuable instrument to be honed and nurtured in service of her art.

When she made her home in Death Valley, Becket fulfilled her early desire for escape to an entirely other world. When she established her own Opera House and trod its boards for 40 years, she fulfilled her early ambitions of an exotic identity and a life fuelled by the imagination. No longer dancing, but still performing, Becket feels vindicated at last by public acclaim, an acclaim that is not just for any single performance or artwork she may have created. While she has sung and danced her way through countless performances of her many acts and routines, she has also been offering a show of 40 years' duration, a dance of life performed against the dramatic canvas of Death Valley that is not lost on her audience. 'Marta's [...] story is the real magic. Patrons of the Amargosa become a part of someone's real-life fairy tale' (Mulvihill 3). As a writer for the *San Francisco Chronicle* put it, Becket 'has worked hard to get where she is today, a relatively unknown artist in the middle of nowhere' who 'loves her unique place in the world'. This may be true, but even so, Becket knows that she has paid a heavy price: 'Life itself is a stage. Millions of plays are going on at once. I didn't realise that I, too, was a part of this drama. I was too busy observing and recording it' (2007: 32).

References

Barthes, Roland. *Camera Lucida*. Trans. Richard Howard. London: Vintage Books, 2000.

Becket, Marta. *Marta Becket—A Theatrical Portrait—Before the Amargosa Opera House*. Death Valley Junction, CA: The Amargosa Opera House, 1998.

———. *Marta Becket—A Theatrical Portrait: The Artist, The Performer And Her Amargosa Opera House*. Death Valley Junction, CA: The Amargosa Opera House, 2003.

———. *To Dance on Sands—The Life and Art of Death Valley's Marta Becket*. Las Vegas: Stephens Press LLC, 2007.

Berry, Oliver. 'Cultural Desert.' *Guardian* <http://www.guardian.co.uk/travel/2002/jun/01/culturaltrips.unitedstates > Accessed June 1 2007.

Du Bois, W E B. *The Souls of Black Folk: Essays and Sketches*. 1903. Cutchogue, NY: Buccaneer Books, 1976.

Findley, Rowe. 'Death Valley—The Land and the Legend.' *National Geographic* 137(January 1970): 1.

Flinchum, Robin. 'The Magic of Marta Becket.' *Pahrump Valley Times* 11 Nov. 2005 <http://archive.pahrumpvalleytimes.com/2005/11/11/news/becket.html>.

Genette, Gérard. *Paratexts: Thresholds of Interpretation*. Trans. Jane E Lewin. Cambridge: Cambridge University Press, 1997.

Lacan, Jacques. 'The Mirror Stage as Formative of the Function of the *I*.' *Écrits: A Selection*. Trans. Alan Sheridan. London: Routledge Classics, 2007: 1–8.

Lejeune, Philippe. *On Autobiography*. Minneapolis: University of Minnesota Press, 1989.

Mulvihill, John. 'Lost Highway Hotel.' <http://davidlynch.de/amargosa.html > Accessed 30 December 2008.

National Park Service. US Department of the Interior. *Death Valley*. <http://www.nps.gov/deva/historyculture/people.htm & http://www.nps.gov/deva/historyculture/the-lost-49ers.htm > Accessed 31 February 2010.

Robinson, Todd, dir. *Amargosa* , 2000.

Schwyzer, Elizabeth. 'Documentary Chronicles Marta Becket's 40-Year Solo Career.' *Santa Barbara Independent* 26 June, 2008 http://www.independent.com/news/2008/jun/26/marta-becket.

Smith, Sidonie and Watson Julia. *Reading Autobiography - A Guide for Interpreting Life Narratives*. Minneapolis and London: University of Minnesota Press, 2001.

Recomposing Her History: the Memoirs and Diaries of Ethel Smyth

Amanda Harris

The published memoirs and unpublished diaries of English composer, writer and feminist Ethel Smyth (1858–1944) can be seen as sites for dissent from public portrayals of her life and career. Smyth's prolific autobiographical writing, appearing across nine published volumes (1919–1940) produced a narrative of rebellion against the male culture of musical life from which she was excluded as a female composer. Her diaries (1918–1941) show a development from early private reflections on personal and emotional experiences to later documents which appear to be written with an audience in mind. I argue that the diaries come to present an important form of life writing for Smyth, painting a controlled portrait of her as creative entity. They further act as a historical record which might outlast her and provide an authoritative account of her life for future researchers. In combination, the memoirs and diaries can be seen as Smyth's project of dissent against the musical press's representation of her as a 'lady composer' rather than a 'composer amongst composers'.

[I]t seems to be generally believed—that her books will do more than her music to preserve and brighten her fame, and that she will ultimately rank as a brilliant author and remarkable character who also made some stir by composing music on an ambitious scale for a woman... (McNaught 110)

The composer, writer and feminist Ethel Smyth (1858–1944) was as prolific a writer of books as she was a composer of music, and her considerable published memoirs have long been used as a source of biographical facts by musicologists studying her music and her life. However, the role of writing in her broader career is only just beginning to be the subject of scholarly enquiry (Unseld 108–20). Smyth devoted many pages of her published memoirs to recounting stories of her tireless efforts to get her works performed and to convincing sceptics that her music should be taken as seriously as any man's. In the memoirs, she maintained a controlled portrait of her skill and professionalism as a composer, rarely acknowledging weakness or fault in her own abilities and behaviour and relentlessly arguing the prejudice of gender and nationality to explain any disjuncture between this portrait and that painted in the press by others. In this sense, the memoirs served the musical career for which she wished to be widely known.

In her unpublished diaries, Smyth wrote about some of the experiences too personal to publish, and she developed ideas for tales that would be included in the published books. In this article, I explore Smyth's writing and the role it played in dissenting from portrayals of her personality and her career in the music press and in emerging books on British composers; in doing so, I consider some of the ways that her writing was intimately connected to her identity as a composer of music. I also consider Smyth's diaries in the context of other scholarship on women's diary writing. The transition in Smyth's diaries from private expressions of emotion to documents which appear to be written with an audience in mind makes them an interesting case study for the discourse on the public and private in women's writing in the early twentieth century. Dannielle Orr is just one contributor to these discussions who has classified the problems of identifying nineteenth-century women's diaries as private pastimes or more dangerous acts of self-preservation (Orr 204). In exploring the ways in which Smyth exercised control over her life through her writing, I engage with these problems of interpretation of unpublished documents.

As a composer, Smyth wrote music across several genres and arguably in numerous styles. She is perhaps best known for her operas, the early works (*Fantasio, Der Wald*) following the grand Germanic opera tradition of her training in Leipzig and the later works which could be seen as attempts to found or at least contribute to a modern English opera tradition (in particular *The Wreckers* and *The Boatswain's Mate*). However, her compositional style is difficult to define partly because of what seems to be her stylistic opportunism. Her 1908 chamber songs reflect the Parisian compositional style their premiere audience would have appreciated, and indeed, Debussy had high praise for their musical contribution (Debussy 42–44). As Smyth wrote later in life, she was willing to try just about anything:

> [I]n the intervals of operatic adventures abroad every sort of ammunition was turned out wherewith to attack our own strongholds ... short choral works, orchestral and chamber works, songs; everything, I think, except a Reverie for Pianoforte and Comb—a regrettable omission, for that might have done the trick. (As Time Went *On* 291–2)

In the context of this musical opportunism then, it is possible to see her writing as an opportunity that she came to regard not as merely complementary to her music but as essential to its survival into posterity.

Smyth's writing can be organised into four distinct categories: published memoirs; published writing including biographies of acquaintances and political polemic; unpublished diaries; and unpublished letters. In this paper, I focus on the role played in Smyth's creative life and in her dissent from public portraits of her by others, by two particular kinds of life writing: published memoirs and unpublished diaries. Smyth wrote 10 books and almost all of them contain some autobiographical component. Published between 1919 and 1940, the books, many of which are specifically labelled as memoirs, are written in an explicitly candid style, juxtaposing tales of heartbreak and impropriety with accounts of her musical life and telling the most personal stories with humour and without shame.

The Memoirs

Smyth was drawn to write her memoirs when she found herself in a situation in which it was impossible to think of music. During the First World War, she volunteered with a radiography unit in Vichy and realised it was not feasible to contemplate composing amongst the noise of constant bombardments. Instead, she began to sketch memories of her life from the end of the nineteenth century, eventually publishing the product in 1919 as *Impressions That Remained*. Encouraged by her French acquaintances' praise of her memoir and their encouragement to continue writing, memoir writing became a substitute for composing music and one which satisfied Smyth's desire for a creative outlet. In the midst of her wartime posting, she wrote in her diary on 13 January 1918: 'I daresay I shall [publish more memoirs], as here I can do nothing else' (*Diary* 12).

This creative output also had a pragmatic side, and writing became an alternative career for Smyth, one by which she could support herself financially. However, beyond the benefits of creative expression and financial stability, for Smyth, writing was motivated by a political imperative to retell a version of her life dissenting from the versions recorded in the media and history books. Or as Smyth explained it, in writing by others:

> I found myself be-hung with a label—that innocent-looking label that has been the bane of my life, from which I have not yet shaken myself free! I was not a composer amongst composers, but a *lady* composer. And as, of course, no woman could possibly write music of her own, it became a habit never to mention mine without reference to some plagiarised victim—Bach, Mozart, Beethoven, Brahms, or Wagner, according to the writer's fancy... If your work has only relative value why should conductors take the trouble to perform it? If it is never performed how can you blame the Press for considering it negligible? and if, owing to all this, you can't get it published—Checkmate! No doubt other English composers have had their difficulties, but once a man gets his head above water he can turn on his back and float. I have struggled to the surface half a dozen times, only to be dragged under again by the dead weight of all the label stands for. ('A Burning of Boats' 384–5)

This defense of her worth as a composer is one of many such excerpts included in Smyth's published writing. Such vehemently argued passages reveal one of the purposes of writing in the context of Smyth's career: it was not just a diversion from composing, but rather was an intervention into what she viewed as the ongoing neglect of her music. As a practice, it was designed to present a portrait of its subject as an accomplished musician, master composer and subject of the admiration of others. Indeed, this project of Smyth's seems, to have been largely successful. Looking back on almost 10 years of writing about her life and music, Smyth acknowledged in 1928 the significant role that her writing career, for which she had become quite famous, had played in the performance of her musical works. She wrote: 'but for having published two volumes of Memoirs in 1919, my work would be as seldom played to-day as it was then' (*A Final Burning of Boats* 16). Two years after this, she suggested that if anyone had heard of her at all as a composer, it was because of her writing ('Dame Ethel Smyth' 87).

Indeed, Smyth's assertions of neglect were not ungrounded. Although she was included in several accounts of British contemporary music, her contribution was consistently marginalised in relation to her male colleagues. An example of this, representative of other publications of its kind, was Joseph Holbrooke's book *Contemporary British Composers* published in 1925. Holbrooke clearly structured his survey of British music to indicate the composers he considered important. His book was organised in a series of 21 chapters, each dealing with a particular male composer. After these, and following a further chapter entitled 'Some Others', was the chapter on 'Women Composers'. In spite of the fact that almost the entirety of this chapter was devoted to Smyth, with only passing mentions of Cécile Chaminade, Dorothy Howell and Rebecca Clarke, the lack of her name in the chapter title implied a lesser importance than the composers recognised by name (Holbrooke 293).

It is thus significant that in contrast with portraits of her by others, in her memoirs, Smyth maintained a stable portrait of her professional persona. Although many personal stories were related, when it came to her professional life, Smyth's talent, determination and ability were never in doubt. She contrasted negative reactions to her gender with solid praise from eminent musicians who appreciated her music in spite of her being a woman. She accounted for the instances where her music was dismissed with gender analysis.

The Diaries

In the diaries, a more nuanced perspective on this expert composer persona is evident. In the early years, the diaries were a location for Smyth to express emotions and self-portraits quite different to those that she published; however, as the years went on, the purpose and intent of the diaries changed, and Smyth exercised more conscious control over their contents. Indeed, seen as a series, the diaries were far from being private documents: they were shared with friends and, as I will discuss, seem to have been intended as historical documents which might aid future researchers in understanding her life.

Smyth began keeping a diary in the same period in which she began writing her first volume of memoirs. She seems to have begun the diaries for herself, recording doubts and fears about her creative abilities and some personal sentiments. Indeed, if the memoirs were a forum for Smyth to assert her worth for the recognition of others, then the early diaries were the location for her expressions of self-doubt. In her diaries, the consequences for music due to the effects of the war and of her increasing deafness were vividly expressed. Through her loss of hearing, she had begun to lose sight of the pleasure that music had always brought her, and the expression of these feelings in her diary seemed to become a source of comfort.[1] Through deafness, Smyth's normal solace in music was taken away from her. In letters from earlier in her life, music had acted as a trope to console Smyth for other losses. In one letter to her long-time correspondent and lover, Harry Brewster, she wrote of the way music had the power to replace any desire for physical intimacy:

> I am conscious that the physical warmth & sensuousness that would in periods of mental inactivity take that form gets another sort of incarnation in music notes. (Harris 84, 21 January 1894)

Yet, as Smyth's hearing failed, the diary entries between 1919 and 1921 came to be a location for expressions of self-doubt which contrast starkly with the egotistical focus of the memoirs. Instead of her familiar confidence, Smyth wrote of depression and hopelessness on 3 March 1919:

> I struggle in vain against the growing depression caused by this [ear] trouble - ...For myself I see nothing in life but...enduring unto the End with as little distress to friends etc as may be...Anyhow life has got to be faced somehow, now that I see that nerve-racking conditions of existence & eventual deafness are my lot. I've put all my affairs in order & devoutly hope another attack like the one of last Oct may put an end to it all. The hideous struggles of my life— specially in the last years—including banishment from Germany or rather Austria—have brought me to the end of my reserves. (*Diary* 61–2)[2]

Because her deafness also created a distance between Smyth and her music, she was no longer consoled by composition, and indeed, she began to question her abilities in writing music. On 20 March 1919, she wrote:

> Heard B[oatswain's] Mate yesty. Beecham conducted I hated it, partly because I am now too deaf to hear orchestration well as far off as we were...the fact is R. Korsakoff orchestrates perfectly and I do not. When you are getting deaf you know it by finding a lot of people enunciate badly—so it is with orchestration. I thought my music...restless, over broken up as to rhythm, too microscopic, not enough alloy, i.e. too much detail point—too long in the cupboard scene & so on. How it pleased anyone I cannot think but I know I am morbid about music— specially mine, for my ears almost make life unbearable...I am trying to compose—no inspiration whatever—but it will never come back unless I put my

> self at the task. The booming in the ears stops concentration so I try to write at the piano all the time…nothing good can come of it but one must live somehow…And now <u>no more of that in this book</u>. (*Diary* 64–5)

The final, underlined sentence of Smyth's outpouring of self-doubt in the diary excerpt above indicates that the depth of hopelessness reached was a turning point at which the diaries ceased to be a location for such emotional expressions. Their shift from a private document to a more self-consciously historical one was partly occasioned by Smyth's success as a writer; a change which aroused her from this hopeless state. Unbeknownst to her at the time of writing that entry, her resolve to write no more about her doubts and fears was to coincide with news of her sudden success as an author, a turn of events that gave her a new outlet for her creativity and a means of financial support. A few days after this entry, Smyth recorded her new-found success on 25 March 1919; the publisher, Longmans, had written to announce that her first book had been accepted for publication. This event marked a significant shift in Smyth's identity as a creative artist. The renewed creative energy which arose out of this new career path allowed her to look beyond the trials of deafness and the loss of music:

> This cheers me immensely as am in a mood of thinking all I do quite worthless & myself a fraud gradually finding myself out & wondering how to take the discovery. (*Diary* 65)

The new perspective precipitated by this event was not short-lived, and Smyth continued to improve in mood and self-belief as the months passed. By 15 May 1919, she commented: 'Anyhow I'm much better in myself & everyone thinks I look very well—but I'm facing the worst' (*Diary* 66). And yet in spite of being confronted with the worst physical ailment that might be faced by a musician, Smyth's life writing had begun to fuel her sense of worth. Indeed, it became not just a vehicle for nostalgic reflection on her life, but a means through which Smyth fashioned a new creative persona. The diaries are a format through which we can observe this shift happening 'live' as it were; it can be charted in time through Smyth's entries throughout 1919.

Accordingly, as writing began to be a substitute for composing, the act of writing itself took on a new function in Smyth's life; it was not only a means of earning an income, but became a tool to rectify the neglect of her music and to incorporate politics into her musical perspective. The diaries changed in parallel to the published memoirs; they ceased to be an outlet for doubt and misery and began to take the role of historical record, to be retrospectively corrected, to become an account of a life for posterity. The extent to which writing also began to replace composition as the essence of Smyth's creative identity is revealed in an entry from 2 March 1920 in which Smyth appears almost regretful that an opera of hers is being performed. This success will prevent her from writing an article which was to complain about the dire state of English opera performance and which would earn her a lot of money:

> Beecham is really doing the Wreckers in the Autumn. This will rather interfere with an article I had promised to write for the E. News on the subject of English opera & for which I meant to ask a huge sum! But I may do it all the same— Everyone on all sides is now forever asking me to "write something" & name my price—also Longman wants me to go on, of course, with more "Impressions." (*Diaries* 131)

Smyth's shift from using a diary in which she indulged in personal reflections to one more closely resembling her published writing can be seen in particular throughout her discussions of her romantic relationships. The early years of Smyth's diary writing also coincided with the beginning of an important romantic relationship with the Irish writer, Edith Somerville. Although Somerville does not feature in Smyth's publications, the intensity and all-consuming passion of this relationship are revealed in correspondence between the two women, spanning the period 1918 to 1938. In her early diary entries, Smyth recorded how important this new friendship was to her; on 12 November 1919: 'A great new event. I have made friends with Edith Somerville ... I have had the unhoped-for, undreamed-of fortune to strike ... in my Autumn ... a new & perfect friend' (*Diary* 103).

This unexpected new passion had the effect of further mitigating the despair that Smyth had been experiencing about her hearing and hence, her music. On 1 November 1919, she wrote: 'the wonderful happiness of having found E[dith] ... all this marks a new epoch' (Diary 116). The continuation of this new relationship across the end of 1919 and into 1920 consolidated for Smyth her renewed energy for life, and in January 1920 she wrote:

> The great & wonderful thing is that this year begins, for me, with the sort of woman friend I have been saving up for all my life—& neither was searching for, nor expected ever to find. Hence a new lease of life. (*Diary* 127)

However, these expressive entries about Smyth's new love affair were not continued for long, and in March of 1920 she began to censor her own expressions of personal sentiment in the pages of her diary: 'It is wonderful to be as unutterably happy as I am now a days—Who'd have thought it or expected it? ... And now no more on this personal and un-diaretic note' (*Diary* 131).

Smyth's remark that to write effusively about her happiness in love was, in her words, 'un-diaretic' offers an important insight into the changing function of her diaries. This is confirmed by the fact that in the years following this period, the diaries ceased to record events of emotional importance and became a chronicle of activities and a record of events for future reference. Even by later in the month that the above entry was written, diary entries had become a collection of unsentimental anecdotes about happenings in Taormina (Sicily) where Smyth and Somerville were holidaying. Much like her memoirs, the entries in the ensuing years were far from impersonally written and still hinted at intimate feelings, but the expressions of romantic joy, self-doubt or questions about the direction of Smyth's life no longer appeared.

Indeed, as the diaries continue from 1920 onwards, it is possible to see them as a notebook for the ideas Smyth was sounding out for publication. In the mid- to late-1920s, for example, a vast proportion of entries were preoccupied with Smyth's new perspectives on the gender prejudice she experienced as a composer. From anecdotes in 1925 about the composer Ralph Vaughan Williams' comments that he did not like Smyth's conducting though he had never seen it—a 'bully though a darling' (*Diary* 96–7) through to an entry on 13 March 1928: 'I think men are jealous of my popularity with audiences, choruses, & orchestras' (*Diary* 14), Smyth's theme was developed into a collection of thoughts and stories that would eventually result in the publication of her ideas on 'musical feminism' in *A Final Burning of Boats* (1928) and Female Pipings in Eden (1936).[3]

At some point, Smyth also came to exercise editorial control over the diaries, a fact that is laid bare in the retrospective corrections of early entries. In Smyth's first diary volume (covering 1918–1921) was a note by her from 1938 stating that her brother-in-law had been killed in 1915. In the 1919 section, she recorded the comment: 'I think this must have been my first attempt at a Diary' *(Diary)*. The diaries were also retrospectively cross-referenced, for example when Smyth wrote on 26 September 1920 that she had given up smoking and referred (the reader?) to the entry of 'Vol II Aug 21 1921' (*Diary* 186).

Smyth also recorded aspects of her reflective process in writing and in deciding what was and was not important to include in the diaries. In the second volume (covering 1921–1926), she wrote from July to September 1922: 'All my adventures are in these articles so I won't repeat them here' (30). The turn of phrase implies not only that she was striving for an accurate historical record, but also that she had a reader in mind. In another entry on 7 December 1918, Smyth discussed Mary Salis-Schwabe, who was 'psychic, tho' otherwise very normal & told me some queer things' and made the remark that Salis-Schwabe's experiences had already been documented in the *Psychical Society's* paper, meaning that there was no need for Smyth to document them in her diary (*Diary* 47).

The impression that the diaries are a deliberate recording of a history is strengthened by Smyth's articulation of her process of documentation, as in the entry on 28 October 1922 when she realised that she had neglected to record her friend Toche's (Augustine Bulteau's) death three weeks earlier and went on to document her reactions to the event. Similarly, the turn of phrase on 3 April 1923, 'The death of Sarah Bernhardt reminds me to put down that Edie Craig asked me to meet her mother last month' suggests a conscious selection of the events important to posterity and to an accurate account of the version of the life she wished to record (*Diary* 51). Smyth continued to write in spite of herself, overcoming the inertia of wishing not to write in noting on 29 March 1924 that even though 'it is too tiresome to write up this book . . . it must be done' (*Diary* 73–4).

The retrospective editing of her private document and self-conscious decisions about what most needed to be documented suggest that the diaries were a part of a very specific project of Smyth's. The project of which her memoirs, diaries and published articles were a part attempted to create a version of her life which would account for her history and portray a certain kind of likeness over which she would have editorial control. This kind of control over the written word stood in stark contrast to the many external forces comprising musicians, music administrators, conductors and critics whose co-operation would be required for her to control her music in the same manner.

Memoirs and Diaries as Strategies of Dissent

The tension between the dual functions of Smyth's diaries—on one hand, an expression of the kinds of doubts she would never have published and on the other, a record which she intended to be read by others, makes them an interesting case study for the dichotomy between the public and the private in women's diary writing. Scholars of the diary have debated the public/private nature of women's diary writing for some years now (see Bunkers and Huff; Huff; McCarthy; and Sinor). In particular, Lynn Bloom contrasts the private diary in which authors recorded so little information about the mundane aspects of daily life that the writing seemed almost coded to an external reader, with the diary written for other readers in which characters were backgrounded and there was an overarching narrative (25–8). Indeed, Smyth's private/public dichotomy falls between the cracks of Bloom's definitions; before she constrained her impulses to vent her despair and fear, the pages of Smyth's early diaries were unwieldy and lack the humour and artfulness of her published writing style. By contrast, once the decision was made to write only what was appropriate to the diary format (by this we might understand publishable diary format), Smyth's diaries began to resemble her published memoirs in their loosely connected series of anecdotes and colourful characterisations of key players in her story. Her diaries are an illuminating example of the slippage between the public and the private in women's diary writing.

In the context of Smyth's re-composition of her life story, the two forms of writing can be seen to be two sides of an attempt to create a dissenting version of her life for posterity. The memoirs, intended as an authoritative source that would convince the public of Smyth's value as a composer, were designed to have an impact on the current reality of her life. The diaries, containing more nuanced reflections, but still maintaining a controlled portrait of Smyth as creative entity, were designed as a historical record which might outlast her and provide an authoritative account of her life for future researchers.

Smyth's diaries are, then, an important historical source for understanding her life and approach to career. Rather than offering an intensely private and personal perspective on the events which appear in her published writings, the diaries present an alternative view of Smyth's professional motivations and a restrained insight into important relationships and events in the final decades of her life. The significant change in her outlook on life following her loss of hearing, which coincided with the publication of her first book, is indicative of how central writing was to the recovery of her creative persona. The shift in the diaries from a private chronicle of woes to the notebook of a writer fit for public consumption is significant when correlated to the published memoirs being penned at the same time. Both forms of writing became evidence of the consistent attempts made by Smyth to leave an account of herself which would dissent from and moderate public representations of her in the media and in music histories. Viewed in parallel, the memoirs and the diaries provide an important insight into the project of creating a historical record that preoccupied Smyth throughout her life and that allowed her to continue beyond the loss of her ability to appreciate music.

Notes

[1]   A recent article by Elizabeth Wood explores Smyth's anxiety about her loss of hearing (36–69).
[2]   All unpublished diaries and letters by Ethel Smyth are copyright of the Ethel Smyth estate and appear with permission.
[3]   These ideas had also been developed in print in several of Smyth's earlier articles ('Reflections on Prejudice'; 'A Burning of Boats').

References

Bloom, Lynn Z. '"I Write for Myself and Strangers": Private Diaries as Public Documents.' *Inscribing the Daily: Critical Essays on Women's Diaries*. Ed. Suzanne L. Bunkers, and Cynthia Anne Huff. Amherst: University of Massachusetts Press, 1996: 23–37.

Bunkers, Suzanne L., and Cynthia Anne Huff, eds, *Inscribing the Daily: Critical Essays on Women's Diaries*. Amherst: University of Massachusetts Press, 1996.

Debussy, Claude. 'Concerts Colonne. - Société des Nouveaux Concerts.' *Revue Musicale S.I.M* 9/12: 42–4.

Harris, Amanda. 'The Smyth-Brewster Correspondence: a Fresh Look at the Hidden Romantic World of Ethel Smyth.' *Women and Music: A Journal of Gender and Culture* 14: 72–94.

Holbrooke, Joseph. *Contemporary British Composers*. London: Cecil Palmer, 1925.

Huff, Cynthia Anne. 'Reading as Re-Vision: Approaches to Reading Manuscript Diaries.' *Biography* 23.3: 505–23.

McCarthy, Molly. 'A Pocketful of Days: Pocket Diaries and Daily Record Keeping among Nineteenth-Century New England Women.' *The New England Quarterly* 73.2: 274–96.

McNaught, William. 'Dame Ethel Smyth, April 23, 1858–May 9, 1944.' *The Musical Times* 85.1217 (1944): 110.

Orr, Dannielle. '"I Tell Myself to Myself": Homosexual Agency in the Journals of Anne Lister (1791–1840).' *Women's Writing* 11.2 (2004): 201–22.

Sinor, J. *The Extraordinary Work of Ordinary Writing: Annie Ray's Diary*. Iowa City: University of Iowa Press, 2002.

Smyth, Ethel, and Henry B. Brewster. *Correspondence* (1892–1908). Unpublished. Private Brewster Family Collection held in Florence, Italy.

Smyth, Ethel, and Edith Œ. Somerville. *Correspondence* (1919–1938). Unpublished. Special Collections, Queen's University Library, Belfast.

Smyth, Ethel. *Diary* (1918–1942). Unpublished. Special Collections, Harlan Hatcher Graduate Library, University of Michigan.

———. *Impressions that Remained*. New York: Da Capo Press, 1981.

———. 'Reflections on Prejudice.' *Music Bulletin* 5.33 (1923): 80–1.

————. 'A Burning of Boats.' *London Mercury* 9.52 (1924): 381–93.

————. *A Final Burning of Boats*. London: Longmans, Green and Co, 1928.

————. 'Dame Ethel Smyth.' *More Points of View: A Second Series of Broadcast Addresses*. London: George Allen & Unwin, 1930: 87.

————. *Female Pipings in Eden*. Edinburgh: Peter Davies Limited, 1934.

————. *As Time Went On...* London: Longmans, Green and Co, 1937.

————. *A Fresh Start*. Unpublished manuscript. Special Collections, Harlan Hatcher Graduate Library, University of Michigan, 1941.

Unseld, Melanie. 'Identität durch Schreiben: Ethel Smyth und ihre autobiographischen Texte.' *Felsensprengerin, Brückenbauerin, Wegbereiterin. Die Komponistin Ethel Smyth*. Ed. Cornelia Bartsch, Rebecca Grotjahn and Melanie Unseld. Munich: Allitera Verlag, 2010. 108–20.

Wood, Elizabeth. 'On Deafness and Musical Creativity: the Case of Ethel Smyth.' *Musical Quarterly* 92.1–2: 36–69.

The Laws of God and Men: Eliza Davies' *Story of an Earnest Life*

Sarah Ailwood

This article explores Eliza Davies' 1881 autobiography *The Story of an Earnest Life* through the lens of nineteenth-century spiritual autobiographic genres. It analyses Davies' use of the spiritual autobiography to create a subjectivity beyond the culturally-sanctioned role of wife and mother, a sense of self that is closely linked to her legal identity. In South Australia in the early 1840s, Davies found herself trapped in a position of legal non-subject through her marriage to a violent, alcoholic husband. Her autobiography charts not only her spiritual journey as Christ's missionary, but also he recreation as a legal subject through the divorce proceedings she brought against her husband in the 1860s. Through her interrogation of legal identity, Davies registers a dissenting voice in contemporary religious and imperial discourses regarding women's social and legal position.

In 1881, Eliza Davies reflected on her 'life of many vicissitudes' (iii) and published her autobiography, *The Story of an Earnest Life: A Woman's Adventures in Australia, and in Two Voyages Around the World*, convinced that it was 'my duty to write' (iii). Published in the hope that 'my readers may derive strength from it under trials, temptations, pain, privation, persecution, and exposure' (iii), and dedicated to the pupils of the Kentucky Female Orphan School where she then taught, Davies uses the individualism and empowerment of Victorian spiritual autobiographic genres to produce a tale of personal victory over adversity. While it may appear formulaic, however, Davies' autobiography exploits subjectivities created through spiritual autobiography to chart not only her physical and spiritual journeys, but also her journey from legal subject to legal non-subject and back to legal subject again. In presenting legal status as linked to identity,

Davies articulates a dissenting voice regarding the legal subjection of married women in nineteenth-century Australia.

Eliza Davies was born Eliza Arbuckle in Scotland in 1821. Her autobiography describes her childhood as a time of emotional estrangement from her mother, a gulf that widened after her conversion to the Scottish Baptist church during her adolescence. In 1838, she left Scotland for New South Wales following a dispute with her mother over an arranged marriage to an older man. In Sydney, she met Charles Sturt and his family and travelled with them to Adelaide, where she was among the first settler group to navigate the Murray. In 1840, at the urging of Mrs Sturt, she married William Davies, a local tinsmith by whom she was physically and emotionally abused and socially isolated. With the support of a local Baptist church, she escaped her violent, alcoholic husband and returned to New South Wales in 1842. Davies eventually returned to Scotland and in 1847 underwent a spiritual conversion during a sermon preached by the American Alexander Campbell. Davies resolved to dedicate her life to spreading his message and fostering the evangelical churches of Christ. She travelled to America with Campbell and remained there until 1858, when she returned to Australia with the view of spreading Campbell's philosophy and distributing the works of the American Bible Union. Her missionary work was focused on education for girls and women. She returned to Adelaide in 1861 and, discovering that her husband was still living, successfully brought divorce proceedings against him in the South Australian Supreme Court. She remained in Australia teaching and preaching Campbell's message until her return to America in 1874, when her autobiography concludes.

When it was published in 1881, *The Story of an Earnest Life* does not seem to have made a particularly substantial impact, and public interest in the work seems to have been confined to reviews in Christian periodicals. Both the book and the writer, however, had a curious afterlife in Jane Sarah Doudy's historical novel *The Magic of Dawn: Sturt's Explorations* published in 1924. Janette Hancock argues that this novel drew substantially on *Story of an Earnest Life* in relation to the Sturt voyage up the Murray (240). Bizarrely, however, this fictional account concludes with the central character Elsie, based on Eliza, marrying not the drunk and violent William Davies but instead a prosperous landowner with whom she lives happily ever after.

At more than 550 pages, the length of *Story of an Earnest Life* itself suggests that Davies was confident in the importance of her story. The text is driven by plot, as Davies recounts her journeys and encounters with those who variously assist, challenge and resist her and the message she brings. As Joy Hooton argues in *Stories of Herself When Young*, Davies perceives 'herself as the central figure in a long-running melodrama' (56). Hooton describes Davies as 'a purveyor of the sensational' (56) and 'totally self-absorbed' (58), and *Story of an Earnest Life* as 'a Gothic romance peopled with villains and angels', composed of 'sinister events, supernatural incidents, disasters, near-disasters, storms, violent deaths and accidents' (57). Indeed, the text's melodramatic tone, religious orientation and views on both indigenous Australians and slavery in southern America make it in many respects unpalatable to a contemporary readership. Yet through her exploitation of autobiographical genres available to Victorian women writers, Davies constructs a self that is complex, occasionally contradictory and constituted through both religious and legal identities. Furthermore, her revelations regarding domestic violence, divorce and the legal subjection of women are strikingly modern.

Published when Davies was 60, *Story of an Earnest Life* allows her to reflectively interpret her life and its events. In *A Poetics of Women's Autobiography*, Sidonie Smith describes a process through which women auto-biographers retrospectively constitute their 'selves' in text:

> As she examines her unique life and then attempts to constitute herself discursively as female subject, the autobiographer brings to the recollection of her past and to the reflection on her identity interpretative figures...Those figures are always cast in language and are always motivated by cultural expectations, habits, and systems of interpretation pressing on her at the scene of writing. (47)

At the 'scene of writing' of *Story of an Earnest Life*, Eliza Davies draws on a wide range of 'interpretive figures', including the established autobiographical modes of the spiritual autobiography and the missionary memoir in addition to fictional genres associated with romance, travel and adventure. The self Davies constructs is simultaneously Christian missionary and martyr, fearless pioneer, victimised wife and romantic heroine. She relentlessly pursues Christ's work despite repeated episodes of physical weakness, unconsciousness and life-threatening illness; she is endangered by numerous perils at sea and on land but is always under God's protecting hand; she is pursued by countless suitors despite being both married and a disciple of Christ.

This multifarious self results in part from Davies' 'hermeneutic freedom', a phrase Smith uses to describe some women's interpretations of their lives away from conventional fictions of womanhood associated with domesticity and the domestic memoir in particular (134). Linda Peterson argues that many Victorian women turned to the domestic memoir genre because the 'memoir—domestic in its focus, relational in its mode of self-construction—allowed women to write as mothers, daughters, wives. It allowed them to interpret their lives in terms of "good" feminine plots' (20). Smith argues that women who achieved herme-neutic freedom, such as Harriet Martineau, used 'an alternative interpretative pattern' to 'escape the tyranny of cultural fictions condemning women to cultural insignificance and silence' (134) associated with domesticity. Married but denied the culturally-approved feminine roles of wife and mother by her husband's violent alcoholism, Davies rejects the Coventry Patmore 'angel in the house' model of womanhood and its generic parallel, the domestic memoir. In its place, she turns her hermeneutic freedom to interpreting her life away from such gendered constraints, drawing instead on models of selfhood associated with Christian missionaries, disciples and martyrs as her central interpretative figures.

Story of an Earnest Life reflects several aspects of spiritual autobiographic genres developed by both male and female writers throughout the Victorian era. In its narrative structure, the text reflects the 'classic' male-orientated spiritual life narrative which Sidonie Smith and Julia Watson argue 'typically unfolds as a journey through sin and damnation to a sense of spiritual fulfilment and arrival in a place of sustaining belief' (205). Many typical features of this genre—including moments of spiritual insight or conversion, episodes of rebellion against established religious institutions, clashes with worldly authority and perse-cution—are present. For example, Davies describes her conversion to the Baptist church in the following terms:

> I suddenly raised my eyes from the bright spot on the pavement, and, looking upward, I saw a bank of pure white, fleecy clouds, and in bold relief was hung a human figure, nailed to a cross, the lower part concealed by the clouds. The sublime beauty of that face surpassed everything I had ever seen or imagined; the large, love-lit eyes, full of pity, penetrated my very soul, and, as I have said, inspired me with hope and joy and peace. (39)

Davies' resistance to established institutionalised forms and practices—regard-less of denomination—is a recurring theme within the text and a core part of her missionary journey. Her indebtedness to spiritual autobiography is clear from her early reference to John Bunyan's *A Pilgrim's Progress*: 'I did not understand the design of the book, but it kept me spellbound till I had heard all of his dream read' (29).

In adopting this traditional formulation of the spiritual autobiography, Davies appears to be unusual among women writers of the Victorian era. Peterson argues that while 'women wrote and published significant numbers of spiritual autobiographies from the mid-seventeenth to early eighteenth century, by the nineteenth such women autobiographers had virtually disappeared from public view' (20) and that women with a religious orientation instead wrote spiritual diaries or domestic memoirs. Indeed, the genre sits uneasily with the strongly gendered self Davies constructs. For example, biblical typology—'the system of finding in the Bible parallels to or patterns in one's own life' (Peterson 84)—used by male spiritual autobiographers as a key interpretative trope through which to constitute a self, is largely unavailable to Davies because of the dearth of female biblical figures who can give meaning to her experience. Davies' use of biblical typology is limited to two female figures. In describing her conversion to the teachings of Alexander Campbell, Davies likens herself to Mary of Bethany: 'O if I could only sit at the feet of this great teacher, as did Mary of Bethany sit at the feet of her Lord, I would be willing to sacrifice anything, everything' (242). Later, she likens her missionary work around Kiama to Phoebe's work in the early Christian church: 'Phebe of Cesarea was commended by Paul to the church at Rome. The Christians were to help her in her business whatever she needed. But the men of this district think a woman is only fit to work in the stockyard' (375). Her limited use of biblical typology to women who are validated by their faith and missionary work implies a doubt that male figures could offer a relevant or meaningful interpretation of women's spiritual experience.

In her application of biblical typology exclusively to female figures, Davies illustrates Sidonie Smith's argument that women 'could not bring to the writing of a spiritual autobiography the same kind of interpretative figures and speaking postures as could their male counterparts' (Smith 133). Smith argues that 'while the biblical tradition offered a template for individual conversion and spiritual growth, it could not clear a space for the figure of an empowered female selfhood' (133). For Davies, the biblical tradition failed not only in its limited models of empowered female selfhood, but also in its models of victimised female selfhood. On the night of her final flight from her husband, Davies experiences a temporary loss of faith that results directly from her vulnerable female position: 'I told Jesus that he could not sympathize with me, because he was not a woman. He was not tempted as I was; He was never situated as I then was' (197). It seems that Davies looked to biblical models both during her life and as she reflected on it when writing her autobiography years later. Yet the biblical tradition cannot offer a model of female subjectivity through which she can authentically interpret her life, represent her experience and construct a model of female selfhood in text.

A more comprehensive model of female selfhood was available to Davies in the form of spiritual autobiography popularised by missionary women in the 1830s and 1840s, described by Linda Peterson as the 'missionary memoir' (84). Peterson argues that the autobiographies of women such as Ann Hasseltine Judson, Sarah Hall Boardman and Margaret Wilson, who 'had gone unofficially to India and whose lives and work were widely publicized in memoirs' (93), 'developed a new form of Victorian life writing, one that represented women taking heroic action, women engaged in serious work outside the home' (97). This genre offered women whose experience did not reflect the culturally-approved roles of wife and mother a model for reflectively interpreting their lives that was sanctioned by Christian and imperial ideologies. However, as Peterson argues, writers of missionary memoirs used the genre to prosecute feminist causes, such as women's education, rights and opportunities (93–5), and to present an empowered female self:

> Women missionaries devoted large sections of their journals and histories to work—in education, in language acquisition and translation, in home visitation and medical aid. Although such accounts of work sometimes sink under heavy religious rhetoric ... these life histories nonetheless give prominence to women's achievements beyond maternity and domesticity. (99)

Peterson's description of the heroic mode in which women missionaries constructed themselves—'braving long ocean voyages, enduring physical hardships of life on mission posts, living without the companionship of English-speaking women, facing customs and practices that would have shocked their European counterparts' (97)—strongly resembles the narrative and tone of *Story of an Earnest Life*.

Davies' account of opening a small school and living in the community at Kiama illustrates her primary narrative focus on work, education and spreading Campbell's message, despite hardship and resistance. She describes her solitary arrival at Kiama: 'Myself, bag and baggage, were left outside the hut on the hillside. There I sat in the midst of all my worldly goods, on a carpet of emerald under a canopy of sapphire' (360). She describes her labour to make the hut habitable: 'I was busy for a whole week trying to get the dirt out of the hut, and fit up a room to sleep in . . . I papered with waste paper the openings between the slabs, to keep out the daylight and moonlight, and wind and rain, and then lined the walls with white cotton, and ceiled it with the same' (361). She describes her students and lessons in detail, relates her various interactions with local clergymen and pseudonymously publishes articles in the local newspapers about current issues and particularly the education of girls (400–1).

Spiritual genres beyond the domestic memoir enabled Victorian women to retrospectively construct an active, empowered female self and to pursue feminist causes relating to women's education, rights and opportunities. Peterson describes 'the use of spiritual autobiography by Victorian women writers' as 'a polemical and political act, a choice signalling public intentions, not just private confessions' (16), and Smith argues that 'intellectual women began to appropriate bits and pieces of traditions, philosophical ideas, and political ideologies that best served their struggle toward a fuller selfhood' (133). This exploitation of spiritual autobiographic genres for more public, political and ideological purposes is evident in Davies' *Story of an Earnest Life*, not only in her educational mission but also as her construction of self interrogates the legal position of married women in the nineteenth century.

In *Story of an Earnest Life*, the law of married women is both a political cause and an alternative trope through which Davies interprets her life and constructs a variously victimised or empowered female self. Issues of law and legal rights and responsibilities recur throughout the text as Davies links legal status to identity. Her legal threats against the owners of a ship who mislead and mistreat her, her determination to understand the legal transactions involved in the establishment of a school at North Sydney and her resentment at using lawyers and other professionals to act on her behalf are marks of her determined individualism, her sense of herself as independent citizen. As Margaret Thornton argues, the assertion of legal rights is 'a means by which active citizens are produced' (335). By far the most important legal narrative in *Story of an Earnest Life*, however, is Davies' journey from legal subject to legal non-subject and back to legal subject again. As a woman married in the colony of South Australia in the nineteenth century, Eliza Davies was initially oppressed and later empowered by law. The legal identities Davies constructs in tandem with her spiritual journey and her missionary work are equally important to her construction of self and rendered in similarly heroic terms. *Story of an Earnest Life* is simultaneously a cry for law reform (regarding the legal subjection of married women) and a testament to the empowerment that law reform can bring (through the introduction of divorce legislation in the mid-nineteenth century). In foregrounding the relationship between legal status and selfhood, Davies exposes the legal and physical subjugation of married women, their difficulties in accessing law and justice and the emotional and personal costs of confronting an oppressor within the justice system.

When Eliza Davies married William Davies in 1840, she effectively became a legal non-subject. As a married woman, she did not have the power to own property, to contract or conduct business or to sue or be sued in her own name. She no longer possessed 'legal personality'; that is, she was no longer recognisable to the law as a person. Instead, under the doctrine of *feme covert* her identity was merged with that of her husband in the eyes of the law. This legal fiction was exported to the common law world, including South Australia, through William Blackstone's *Commentaries on the Law of England*: 'By marriage, the husband and wife are one person in law: that is, the very being or legal existence of the woman is suspended during the marriage, or at least is incorporated and consolidated into that of the husband; under whose wing, protection, and cover, she performs every thing' (85).

Davies' position as legal non-subject renders her all the more vulnerable in her descriptions of the domestic violence she suffered:

> He, with a strong, outstretched arm, pushed me back to my seat, and without one word spoken, or warning given, he struck me several heavy blows on the head with his heavy-heeled boot. I thought my brains were being knocked out. I gave one cry for mercy from the infuriated man, but he had none. I cried to God to save me. The boot that battered my head to jelly almost was caught in the window curtain, as it was raised with a fearful oath to give the finishing stroke. The curtain was torn down, and flared out the light, and we were in total darkness. I sat with the curtain in my mouth to smother my cries. (176)

> Just then a rough hand was laid on my shoulder, and I was dragged unresistingly to the house, my bonnet and dress torn off me, and a thick rope, knotted and twisted, was whirled about my head and bare shoulders till I had no strength left to stand up under the blows. I fell back on a sofa unconscious, and there lay till the next day. (178)

Davies' publication of such graphic descriptions of domestic violence itself registers a voice of dissent in nineteenth-century imperial ideologies of marriage and domesticity. Arriving in the colony as a single woman in 1838, Davies appears to be part of the mass exportation of unmarried women of 'virtuous character' from Britain to New South Wales throughout the 1830s (Oxley 173). Such women were expected to work as domestic servants and later marry and settle into comfortable domesticity in the new colony, and this is exactly the path Davies sought to follow. Yet, as Hilary Golder and Diane Kirkby argue: 'Coverture and the common law gave husbands the right to beat and the right to control economically ... wife-beating was widespread and taken for granted in nineteenth-century Australia' (156). While there may have been no place for this experience in imperial visions of domesticity, and no space for this voice in the domestic memoir, the spiritual autobiography allows Davies to construct a self outside such ideologies; one that is both independent of and victimised by her husband. By offering Davies a more complete model of individualised selfhood, spiritual autobiography makes possible the expression and publication of experience otherwise suppressed within Victorian culture.

Although at the time of her marriage Davies seems to have reflected only on the religious rather than the legal dimensions of her new relationship, she was keenly aware of her position as legal non-subject during the time she lived with her husband. When he announces a visit to New Zealand on business, Davies informs him of her intention to leave him, but agrees to manage his business in Adelaide until his return as long as he will give her a power of attorney: "'you told me Mrs. –, the merchant's wife, was imprisoned for doing business in her husband's name and absence without one, and I do not wish my services to be rewarded by imprisonment'" (188). In response to Davies' awareness of her need for legal protection, her husband and his friend, a lawyer, conspire to give her a power of attorney that is legally invalid because their signatures are not witnessed. Upon his return to Adelaide, he accuses Davies of 'acting and transacting business in his name, and appropriating all the money I could collect for my own use without his authority' (198) and threatens to prosecute and imprison her if she leaves him—"'I expect you will prefer living with me to going to prison'" (198). Davies asserts her legal position by proving that the power of attorney was in fact witnessed by the local publican, giving her legal protection.

Davies seeks religious rather than legal guidance in both deciding to leave her husband and acting on her decision. Law regulating marriage and divorce in South Australia was effectively a vacuum in 1842. While the English common law had been enforceable in South Australia at least since the establishment of civil courts in 1838, there were no ecclesiastical courts, which under English law had exclusive jurisdiction over voidable marriage, judicial separation and procedures for divorce (Jones 3; Kercher 138). Although Davies was entitled to petition the South Australian Governor and Executive Council for a private divorce bill, in practice such a petition would have been rejected because 'the colonial governors had been instructed by the Colonial Office to withhold their assent' (Jones 8). The policy behind these instructions was to 'keep colonial marriage intact and colonial society stable' (Jones 3), regardless, apparently, of the consequences. There was, therefore, effectively no way by which a marriage could be legally dissolved in South Australia at the time.

In the absence of state-sanctioned legal guidance or redress, Davies turned instead to biblical teachings and the local Baptist church. Ultimately, she reasons that her presence in the house causes her husband to sin, and therefore the best course of action is to leave, preventing his sinful behaviour: 'Were I to leave him he would not have the temptation to sin so fearfully…If through me the offences came, would the Bible sanction my leaving him?' (187). She writes: 'The Bible teaches woman her whole duty to God and man. My duty seemed to stand out in bold relief, and though my heart sank at the thought of facing the dark and frowning world again, yet I must bear the cross and follow the Savior' (191). The local Baptist church conducted a quasi-legal inquiry into her case and ultimately approved her decision and assisted her return to New South Wales. Davies declined prosecuting her husband for ill-treatment, reasoning "'I leave him in God's hands, I shall do him no harm'" (201).

As a married woman, Davies was legally incapable of owning property in her own right, and her husband insisted that she leave everything behind her. She records him as saying "'I have law on my side, and I can, and I think I will, strip you now of all your wardrobe, except what you stand in'" (200). Her reply—"'Well, if the law permits you to do that, do it'"—implies a stoic acceptance of her legal subjugation, but the more melodramatic, "'I ask no consideration or sympathy from you. I will go forth naked, poor, despised, forsaken, friendless and alone, leaning on the arm of omnipotence, rather than ask anything of you, or live with you again'" (200) clearly highlights the injustice of married women's property law.

Twenty years later when she returned to South Australia in 1861, Davies developed quite a different view of leaving her husband in God's hands. Upon discovering that he is still living, Davies consults a lawyer and judge about her legal remedies and is advised that she can commence divorce proceedings against him. She reflects: 'Suddenly a strange new feeling came over me, as though the agency of some hidden power was at work. I felt myself grow strong. Whence this new strange power?' (420). While Davies attributes her strength to God, her newly discovered agency also arises from the *Matrimonial Causes Act 1858* (SA) and the power it gave to victimised wives. This Act made divorce and separation more available by allowing parties to apply through the civil courts rather than petitioning the Governor and Executive Council. The *Matrimonial Causes Act* was heavily biased towards men, who could obtain a divorce by proving their wives' adultery, while women were required to prove both adultery and some other 'degrading circumstance', such as incest, rape, cruelty or desertion. The terms of judicial separation were more equal, with both husbands and wives needing to prove 'adultery, cruelty or desertion for at least two years' (Jones 9). The difference between these—divorce and judicial separation—was that under the former the parties were allowed to remarry, whereas the later action was a mechanism for a financial settlement and provided married women with separate legal status (which then allowed them to contract, own property and keep their income). Because it was easier to prove than divorce, judicial separation was known as the 'woman's remedy' (Golder and Kirkby 157). Davies' decision to apply for divorce rather than judicial separation—which would have been easy to prove—is curious in itself, as Davies repeatedly affirms her resolution to remain single (210); in practical terms, a judicial separation would have been as effective as a divorce. Davies' application to have the marriage utterly dissolved reflects a desire for absolute freedom and reconstruction as an entirely separate legal subject: 'All I prayed for was that the law would not give him dominion over me' (426).

Davies retained the Crown Solicitor, Mr Bakewell, to act in her divorce case, but did most of the investigation and preparation of evidence herself. She dwells on the difficulties she faced in locating witnesses and evidence to prove her case, constructing her assertion of her legal rights in strongly heroic terms: 'It seemed that nothing short of a superhuman effort could trace up evidence of things long past, and perhaps forgotten … If I expected or desired freedom, a heavy task lay before me' (421–2). She reflects on her own determination to achieve liberation: 'There is a power in the human will, when bent with unswerving purpose on one great aim' (422). Her account bears a striking and disturbing resemblance to the experience of contemporary women accessing the legal system to deal with violent husbands and partners in criminal and family law contexts. She struggles to convince witnesses to testify to her husband's cruelty, even after her discovery of his second marriage strengthens her case on the ground of bigamy:

> He seemed alarmed when I told him I wished him to testify to a second marriage.
> I found him very unwilling to answer any more questions. I asked him and his wife
> if they remembered, or did they choose to forget, the cruelty that drove me from
> the colony. (422–3)

Davies' account of the trial itself also reveals the personal and emotional costs of taking legal action against a violent partner that resonates with the experiences of contemporary women. In writing her deposition, she finds herself reliving her trauma: 'while writing of cruel deeds, I seemed to be living in the dark past, with all my dead hopes scattered around me. Tongue cannot tell what torture I suffered while writing that document' (424). She records the sense of alienation she felt in the courtroom itself:

> The Hon. Judge Quinn, in his official robes and huge powdered wig, on the bench.
> The lawyers, in their full white wigs and black gowns, were all very imposing as
> they bent over their important documents. I sat as if I were in a dream. I could
> not realize that I had an important part to act in the drama that was passing
> before me. (424)

Davies dwells on her suffering when forced by judicial process to confront her husband in the courtroom: 'I felt his presence in every nerve of my frame' (424).

Because Davies brought evidence to establish her husband's bigamy, this was itself sufficient to grant her a divorce under the *Matrimonial Causes Act*. This meant, however, that the court did not consider the graphic evidence she presented of the domestic violence she suffered, or her claim on the ground of cruelty. The *South Australian Advertiser* recorded the judgment of the court that 'as the second marriage and cohabitation on the second marriage had been proved, the Court did not think it necessary to enquire into the question of cruelty, that alone being sufficient for a decree' (Tuesday 30 July 1861, 3). In this way, Davies' divorce case reflects the law's disinterest in validating personal experience—particularly of victimisation and trauma—beyond its own very narrow requirements. This does not, however, appear to have been of great concern to Davies herself. She writes: 'When the decision of the Court was written on parchment, signed, sealed and delivered to me, how did I feel? My prayer had been heard and answered by a prayer-hearing and prayer-answering God, and I was legally and morally free' (426). She again declines prosecuting her husband, her use of the law limited to recreating her identity rather than punishment:

> not one hair of this man's head shall suffer on my account. Vengeance or revenge does not belong to me. God knows I forgive him all the injuries he has ever done me. Now that he is in my power, and the law of the land supports me to bring him to punishment, I will show that I have freely forgiven him . . . as soon as I am well enough, I shall leave the colony, and never more cross his path, and may he turn to the Lord, and live in peace. (426)

In concluding her account of resuscitation as a legal person, Davies reminds her reader of the active, empowered role she played in asserting her legal rights:

> In settling accounts with Mr Bakewell, he said, in getting the case up I had done the work of two men, and that what services he had rendered, he cheerfully rendered to me for nothing, as a friend—that I had done the most difficult part of the work, and he had no trouble with the case. (427)

Davies' husband died just a few days after the divorce trial, and she visited his grave:

> My sick soul has darkened with shadows from my past sufferings. The man who had ruined my life, and blighted my happiness, and made my life a hard and bitter thing, lay at my feet. I had in my woman's helplessness to struggle alone against the world in sighs and tears. I have carried a quivering, stricken human heart within me, but all unknown to the world through which I was struggling. (428)

She dwells on the ongoing pain and suffering caused by her traumatic marriage, again registering a voice of dissent in Victorian celebrations of marriage and domesticity.

The individualism of spiritual autobiography—both in its traditional formulation and in the mode of the missionary memoir popularised by early Victorian women—enables Eliza Davies to construct a feminine yet independent and empowered self away from conventional ideas about Victorian womanhood. The law is represented in *Story of an Earnest Life* as variously oppressive and liberating, and Davies as an active citizen within the terms she is offered by it: defiant, resistant, empowered. Davies' exploitation of the subjectivities of spiritual autobiographic genres enables her to construct a self that is constituted in part by the legal identities she inhabits. In so doing, she makes heard a dissenting and little-known voice regarding domestic violence, the legal oppression of women and access to justice in nineteenth-century Australia.

References

Blackstone, William, and John Bethune Bayly. *Commentaries on the Law of England, In the Order, and Compiled from the Text of Blackstone*. London, 1840.
Davies, Eliza. *The Story of an Earnest Life: A Woman's Adventures in Australia, and in Two Voyages Around the World*. Cincinnati, 1881.

Golder, Hilary, and Diane, Kirkby. 'Marriage and Divorce Law Before the *Family Law Act.*' *Sex, Power and Justice: Historical Perspectives of Law in Australia.* Ed. Kirkby. Diane Melbourne: Oxford University Press, 1975, 1995.

Hancock, Janette Helen. 'A Not So Innocent Vision: Re-Visiting the Literary Works of Ellen Liston, Jane Sarah Doudy and Myrtle Rose White.' PhD thesis, University of Adelaide, 2007. Print.

Hooton, Joy W. *Stories of Herself when Young: Autobiographies of Childhood by Australian Women.* Melbourne: Oxford University Press, 1990.

Jones, Helen. *In Her Own Name: A History of Women in South Australia from.* Kent Town: Wakefield Press, 1836, 1994.

Kercher, Bruce. *An Unruly Child: A History of Law in Australia.* Sydney: Allen & Unwin, 1995.

Nettelbeck, Amanda. 'South Australian Settler Memoirs.' *Journal of Australian Studies* 68: 97–104.

Oxley, Deborah. *Convict Maids: The Forced Migration of Women to Australia.* Cambridge: Cambridge University Press, 1996.

Peterson, Linda H. *Traditions of Victorian Women's Autobiography: The Poetics and Politics of Life Writing.* Charlottesville: University Press of Virginia, 1999.

Smith, Sidonie. *A Poetics of Women's Autobiography: Marginality and the Fictions of Self-Representation.* Bloomington: Indiana University Press, 1987.

Smith, Sidonie, and Watson, Julia. *Reading Autobiography. A Guide for Interpreting Life Narratives.* Minneapolis: University of Minnesota Press, 2001.

South Australian Advertiser, Tuesday 30 July 1861

Thornton, Margaret. 'Citizenship, Race and Adjudication'.'*Judicial Power, Democracy and Legal Positivism.* Ed. Tom Campbell, and Jeffrey Goldsworthy. Alderhsot: Ashgate, 2000: 335–54.

She Speaks with the Serpent's Forked Tongue: Expulsion, Departure, Exile and Return

Luz Hincapié

In this piece, I discuss anthropologist Ruth Behar's self-reflexive writing and how it has inspired me to think about my own personal experiences within the context of my research. Behar urges for a writing that is vulnerable—a self-ethnographical writing which takes us somewhere we couldn't otherwise go and moves us to identify intensely with those one is writing about. In this manner, I explore Behar's notion of 'vulnerable writing' to approach issues and experiences from my own life history which inform my research on migration and identity. Expulsion, departure, exile and return—recurrent themes in her writing—have likewise been central in my reflections on my family's experience of migration from Colombia to the United States and have sparked my interest in the migration of Japanese to Colombia. My desire to tackle this little-known episode of Colombian history from the experience and point of view of the descendents of this migration, using life history methodologies, stems from the hope of drawing deep connections between personal experience and the subjects under study, between the responsibility of speaking from the margins and understanding the privileged position I occupy—a position which was the product of my own migration experience.

I. The Serpent's Tongue

There is no agony like bearing an untold story inside you. (Neale Hurston 213)

In their introduction to *Women Writing Culture*, Ruth Behar and Deborah Gordon caution:

> When a woman sits down to write, all eyes are on her. The woman who is turning others into the object of her gaze is herself already an object of the gaze...Clutching her pencil, she wonders how "the discipline" will view the

writing she wants to do. Will it be seen as too derivative of male work? Or too feminine? Too safe? Or too risky? Too serious? Or not serious enough? (2)

Gloria Anzaldúa has a similar concern when she comments, 'Writing is the most daring thing I have ever done and the most dangerous... Writing is dangerous because we are afraid of what the writing reveals... Yet in that very act lies our survival because a woman who writes has power' (Moraga and Anzaldúa 171). Writing, like the biblical apple from the forbidden tree of knowledge, can be dangerous for a woman. It makes her both vulnerable and powerful and can result in expulsion and exile from the paradise of Academia.

For Chicanas Gloria Anzaldúa and Cherríe Moraga, writing is done in innovative ways by combining personal ethnographies with critique, poetry and storytelling. Anthropologist Ruth Behar recognises the influence of these writers who have come to the issue of self-representation in subversively feminist ways:

> From their position straddling selfhood and otherhood, Spanish and English, Mexican identity and *agringado* identity, power and resistance, Chicano and Chicana writers have so radically shifted the terms of cultural analysis that it now seems impossible to imagine doing any kind of ethnography without a concept of borderlands or of border crossings. (*Translated Woman* 15)

The concept of the borderlands is poetically explored by Gloria Anzaldúa in her seminal *Borderlands/La Frontera: The New Mestiza*. In this text, we learn about the Nahuatl deity Coatlalopeuh: 'Coatl' is the word for serpent and 'lopeuh' means 'one who has dominion over serpents' (49–51). For the Olmecs, the text tells us, womanhood was associated with the serpent's mouth, a sort of *Vagina Dentata* from which all things were born (56). The snake goddess, a powerful Mesoamerican symbol, syncretised into the Virgin of Guadalupe. Both Behar and Anzaldúa make use of this imagery when they claim to speak with a forked tongue (Anzaldúa 77).[1]

With a tongue split between Spanish and English, Behar writes about what it means to be an anthropologist, how she came to know others by knowing herself and to know herself by knowing others (*Vulnerable Observer* 33). She insists on a writing that is vulnerable—a self-ethnographical writing which takes us somewhere we couldn't otherwise go and moves us beyond inertia to identify intensely with those one is writing about (*Vulnerable Observer* 14). This paper is a meditation on Ruth Behar's self-reflexive writing and how it has influenced my own. It is an opportunity to write vulnerably about how my life story influences my research on migration and identity. It is also an occasion to acknowledge foremothers such as Behar and Anzaldúa; their dissenting voices forged new ways of writing about Self and Other which are far from a dispassionate and distant authoritative voice. Because of them, I can now fashion a more inclusive voice and use my own forked tongue to speak about migration and return to the imaginary homeland and to writing.

II. Crossing the Border

A borderland is a vague and undetermined place created by the emotional residue of an unnatural boundary. It is a constant state of transition. The prohibited and forbidden are its inhabitants. (Anzaldúa 25)

We cross borders, but we don't erase them; we take our borders with us. (Behar, *Translated Women* 320)

My family was not expelled from Colombia, but our departure was not voluntary either. It was my mother's idea to go to the United States because she had heard there were jobs there. My parents got married young and migrated from their small village to find work in different cities in Colombia. But opportunities were scarce in that era known as 'La Violencia' (literally, The Violence) in the late 1940s and 1950s which set off a bloody bi-partisan war in the countryside that would soon lead to the formation of guerrilla groups, massive migration to the cities and diaspora. By the time I was born, my mother was desperate enough after a life of hardship to consider migration to the United States. She left me—six months old— in the care of her older sister and travelled to a country she knew nothing about. She once told me that back then it sounded like going to the moon.

I imagine my mother's arrival to New York City in the late 1960s, to the city of disco in a country at war, my mother primly dressed looking for the address of the contact who was supposed to help her in that huge city, speaking not a word of English, feeling lost. She found work as a live-in maid for a wealthy Jewish family whose newborn baby reminded her of me too much; she changed work and began to clean office buildings. She held several jobs at a time in order to bring the rest of the family over and to buy a house in Colombia since the initial dream of every immigrant is to eventually return home. My sister and four brothers arrived one at a time and went straight to work while the struggle to bring me over continued.

During my adolescence, I blamed all my unhappiness on that migration. I felt I had been wrenched from paradise, from living in a tiny town in the middle of a mountainous area where children played on the unpaved streets, where fun meant swimming in the river, climbing the mountains or squeezing the syrupy juice out of the sugarcane till your jaws hurt. I lived with my aunt and uncle who spoiled me because they felt sorry that I was not growing up with my real family. Once in a while, a woman would come to the house bringing fantastic gifts until I was told this was my mother and that I would soon go to meet my father. It was spring 1976 when I arrived in New York City; my only memory of that night was the amazing ocean of lights that spread everywhere. But the thrill of seeing my family soon turned into the trauma of being an outsider, not knowing the language, not fitting into the public school system and feeling confined in a small apartment.

We lived in Jackson Heights, Queens—a neighbourhood full of immigrants like us—where the city blocks marked the borderlands of each ethnicity; the smells, colours and sounds of Dominicans, Indians, Mexicans, Chinese, Lebanese and Afro-Americans blended together—the so-called melting pot of this multicultural ghetto. Though a decade later a 'Little Colombia' would emerge, back then we were only a handful of Colombian families in this area where the racist and ethnocentric battles of the larger society were performed in the schoolyard. At home, another battle was being waged between my mother and a rebellious me who blamed her for having brought me over, for being so thankful for this new life, for loving the United States where we had become illegal aliens struggling for more than 15 years to achieve full citizenship. We had become spics, people of colour, discriminated minorities. I would later realise the irony in this when I received a college scholarship named after W. E. B. Dubois *because* I was considered a minority. Another irony was that I was the one who benefited most from the migration, never experiencing the privation and hard work which my siblings had. Instead, I went to university where I began a long process of dealing with the issues of belonging, identity, race and gender which had plagued my teenage years. My undergrad thesis, defiantly written in Spanish and entitled 'Crónica de una familia emigrante' (Chronicle of an Immigrant Family), was a first attempt at making sense of the immigrant experience. In hindsight, that piece of writing which now seems overly naive and sentimental has the virtue of having aroused an interest in migration, identity and diaspora which would later coalesce into a lifetime intellectual project.

More than a decade after writing about my family's immigration, I discovered Ruth Behar's work and was mesmerised by the way she blended academic writing with her personal experience. Although her story was different, her writing spoke to me about my own struggles with two cultures and about my search for identity. Behar's maternal grandparents were Ashkenazi Jews while her paternal grandparents were Sephardic Jews born in Turkey. They arrived to Cuba on a stopover to the United States, but after the 1924 US Immigration and Naturalization Act, the Island became a permanent home for many Jews, at least until the Revolution. Behar highlights the irony of the situation: the same Jews who had been rejected by US immigration laws would now enter the country as Cubans, 'as symbolic capital, as one of the human spoils of the victory of U.S. capitalism over impudent Cuban socialism' ('Juban América' 207). Behar arrived to Queens 15 years before I did and was also told to be grateful: '*Hay que dale, gracias a este país* (we have to thank this country)'[2] her mother would say ('Juban América' 207). I too was reminded that the United States meant opportunity and safety for us; Colombia was instability and poverty, but this didn't stop me from longing for the homeland.

III. The Imaginary Homeland

It may be that writers in my position, exiles or emigrants or expatriates, are haunted by some sense of loss, some urge to reclaim, to look back, even at the risk of being mutated into pillars of salt. But if we do look back... we will not be capable of reclaiming precisely the thing that we lost... we will, in short, create

fictions, not actual cities or villages, but invisible ones, imaginary homelands...
(Rushdie 10)

Soon after I finished my undergraduate studies, I announced to my family that I would be returning to Colombia *for good*. When my family saw me packing for this trip with no return, they started to joke saying 'regresarás con la cola entre las piernas' (you will return with your tail between your legs). This meant that I would not adapt to Colombia—that I would return, repent, and, at last, be grateful to the United States. The idea of returning had been with me all through college, and I was determined to prove them wrong.

The last images of the United States that I took with me were the Gulf War and the Los Angeles Riots which I watched dumbfounded on television. I could no longer take the hypocrisy of this country that was not mine. I thought there had to be another place where I truly belonged, where I could restore, 'an imaginary fullness' to set against a fractured past to use Stuart Hall's words (112). I returned to the homeland in 1992, the year Rigoberta Menchú won the Nobel Peace Prize. Her testimony *Me llamo Rigoberta Menchú y así me nació la conciencia*[3] had first been published a decade earlier. When I read her story in college my own consciousness was awakened to the historical debacle of 500 years of colonisation and neo-colonisation. Still, the Roman Catholic Church wanted to celebrate the evangelisation of the Americas while indigenous peoples were calling for mourning after invasion, exploitation and genocide. The Quincentenary commemoration collapsed amidst growing numbers of protests and counter-events which contested the history and meaning of Columbus's voyage.

As I made my return voyage to the lost homeland, Ruth Behar was returning to hers. She returned to Cuba at the end of 1991 to celebrate the New Year and to discover that the recovery of the lost childhood was easier said than done. She quotes performance artist Carmelita Tropicana to explain this sense of loss:

> I am like a tourist in my own country. Everything is new. I walk everywhere hoping I will recall something. Anything. I have this urge to recognize and be recognized. To fling my arms around one of those ceiba trees and say I remember you... I want a crack in the sidewalk to open up and say, yes, I saw you when you jumped over in your patent leather shoes holding onto your grandfather's index finger. But it doesn't happen. There is no recognition from either the tree or the sidewalk. (Qtd. in *Vulnerable Observer* 141)

Behar returned to Cuba in search of memories of an abandoned childhood which she could not find. She had other lost homelands to recover, and that same year, she embarked on a reverse journey from the New World to Turkey to her grandparents town, Silivri; 'Another mythical place the granddaughter will come to feel her feet must stand upon in this Columbian year, imagining it bears some secret, some knowledge, some deep truth, about herself" ('Story of Ruth' 262–3). She then returns to Spain, from where her Sephardic ancestors had been expelled 500 years earlier.

I also returned to Bogota looking for some deep truth or meaning only to discover the fictions of my identity—to discover how un-Colombian I really was. My struggles with Spanish were evident, but I was not willing to admit that English had become my native tongue. It seemed a sign of defeat confirmed when others called me a *gringa* as they heard me speak. As the myth of my identity and belonging crumbled, I had to agree with Salman Rushdie: the immigrant can never recover the homeland; the best we can do is to create fictions, invisible, imaginary homelands, Cubas and Colombias of our minds. The path back to the imaginary homeland and the lost childhood can only be recovered in narration. This is the value of life writing since it creates forms of embodied knowledge in which the (adult) self and the (child) other can rediscover and reaffirm their connectedness (Behar, *Vulnerable Observer* 134–5). We write about our relationship to the lost homeland, part memory, part forgetting, part longing—a homeland we are not sure we have a right to claim as our own. Arriving to Bogota as an adult, I have no childhood memories there; instead, my memories are from a town called Planadas, as mythical as Silivri is to Ruth Behar.

IV. Cultural Translator

> We want our lives to have meaning, or weight, or substance, or to grow toward some fullness...if necessary we want the future to "redeem" the past, to make it part of a life story, which has sense and purpose, to make it up in a meaningful unity...we must inescapably understand our lives in narrative form, as a quest. (Charles Taylor, qtd. in Plummer 395)

During my eighth birthday celebration right before migrating out of Colombia, I was given a beautiful red diary which I took with me to the United States. Throughout my troubled immigrant adolescence, I accumulated around a dozen of these. Writing was therapeutic and gave meaning to what seemed, after reading much Sartre and Camus, an empty and senseless existence. One day I destroyed each and every diary, throwing away all remnants. As I try to remember when I did this, why I did it, what bothers me now is not the destruction but not remembering where it happened. Was it before leaving the United States? Did I carry those diaries with me to Colombia? Was I trying to erase the whole history of my migration? Was I trying to destroy proof of that fractured identity that made me feel un-whole? Upon return to the homeland, I faced the fact that Identity was not an essence but a process and a positioning, as Stuart Hall explains:

> Far from being grounded in a mere "recovery" of the past which is waiting to be found, and which, when found, will secure our sense of ourselves into eternity, identities are the names we give to the different ways we are positioned by, and position ourselves within, the narratives of the past. (112)

Constructing our narratives through memory, fantasy and myth, we become storytellers. Those of us who live in the borderlands, in the intersection of two or more cultures—in an in-between space—also become cultural translators. In *Translated Woman: Crossing the Border with Esperanza's Story*, Behar is aware of being cultural translator for Esperanza, a Mexican peddler, and of the ethical questions that arise from commodifying her stories into academic text. She questions her role of interviewer, collector, transcriber, translator, academic and peddler of another woman's words (12). By inserting herself into the story with a 'Biography in the Shadow', we are made aware of the historical, economic, cultural and political relations implied in a narrative displaced across many borders.

These are the borders which I must now cross—national, racial and cultural borders—to become translator for the subjects of my PhD dissertation; the descendents of the Japanese immigrants who arrived to Colombia at the beginning of the twentieth century. Because of my interest in the field, I was intrigued by the history of immigration of Japanese to Latin America and the cultural contact between these two regions of the world. My intrigue turned to fascination when I discovered that my country had its own community of Japanese Colombians, one which no one seemed to know about and which barely appeared in historical texts. The initial idea for my doctoral research was to focus on literature and film by Japanese Peruvians and Brazilians, but I soon discovered that there was plenty of scholarly attention on the Japanese diaspora in these countries because it was older and much larger. That there had been a small (close to 200 immigrants) but influential migration of Japanese to the Cauca River Valley in Colombia between the 1910s and 1930s seemed of no consequence to Colombian scholars, with few exceptions.[4]

Once my focus shifted to the Japanese immigration and the descendents in the Cauca River Valley, I began to ask the same questions that have continuously plagued me. How do the Japanese immigrants in Colombia recount their story of immigration, and how do they integrate two very different cultures into a cohesive narrative of identity and belonging? How do they inhabit the border-lands of nation, race, gender and language? With their tongue split between Japanese and Spanish, do they also become cultural translators? Because this was a small and neglected migration, there weren't many texts that I could consult, and for the first time in my academic career, I had to take the leap of faith into the unknown field of ethnographic interviewing. At first, I was petrified with the idea of actually speaking to flesh and blood people, of making mistakes, of not asking the right questions or of being insensitive to their needs and wishes. I soon realised, however, that there was a paradox in my fears—I had already done this! My own family had been the subjects of my interviews for my undergrad thesis, my mother and father patiently telling me painful stories from their past which I recorded, fully aware of their significance. Although back then I had not read much about the ethics or methodologies of ethnographic interviewing, I was conscious of the power of redemption that these life stories could carry. My doubts were eased with this revelation and with the thoughts that there were shared experiences between my interview participants and me; that despite not being of Japanese descent myself, I could relate to their migration experience and to their bicultural condition, that I could write about them the way I wanted to write about my family and myself.

And so I again cross borders to return, this time, to writing about myself from which I was estranged with the obliteration of my diaries. I want to write myself into the text so as to explore shared histories and plural identities which shape both the self and the other and give meaning to life writing. I want to be able to speak—with my forked tongue—about my experience with more detachment and about my research participants with all the fire of feeling in the hope of drawing deep connections. Distrustful of the objective scientific gaze, I want instead to write vulnerably, understanding the responsibility that comes with the privileged position I occupy within the borderlands, a privilege that was the product of my family's migration.

Notes

[1] Behar refers to her forked tongue in her note to the reader in the poetry section of her webpage, accessed 25 October 2009: http://www.ruthbehar.com/Poetry.htm.
[2] Emphasis on the original.
[3] The English translation is entitled *I Rigoberta Menchú and Indian Woman in Guatemala*, but the Spanish title literally means, 'My name is Rigoberta Menchú and thus was my consciousness born'.
[4] See, for example, Sanmiguel.

References

Anzaldúa, Gloria. *Borderlands/La Frontera: The New Mestiza*. San Francisco: Aunt Lute Books, 2007.

Behar, Ruth. 'Juban América.' *King David's Harp: Autobiographical Essays by Jewish Latin American Writers*. Ed. Stephen A. Sadow. Albuquerque: University of New Mexico Press, 1999.

———. *The Vulnerable Observer: Anthropology That Breaks Your Heart*. Boston: Beacon Press, 1996.

———. 'The Story of Ruth, the Anthropologist.' *People of the Book: Thirty Scholars Reflect on their Jewish Identity.* Ed. Shelley Fisher Fishkin, and Jeffrey Rubin-Dorsky. Madison: University of Wisconsin Press, 1996.

———. *Translated Woman: Crossing the Border with Esperanza's Story*. Boston: Beacon Press, 1993.

Behar, Ruth, and Deborah, Gordon. *Women Writing Culture*. Berkeley: University of California, 1995.

Hall, Stuart. 'Cultural Identity and Diaspora.' *Contemporary Postcolonial Theory: A Reader.* Ed. Padmini Mongia. London: Arnold, 1996.

Moraga, Cherríe, and Gloria, Anzaldúa. *This Bridge Called My Back: Writings by Radical Women of Color*. Watertown, MA: Persephone Press, 1981.

Neale Hurston, Zora. *Dust Tracks on a Road, An Autobiography.* Urbana: University of Illinois Press, 1984.

Plummer, Ken. 'The Call of Life Stories in Ethnographic Research.' *Handbook of Ethnography*. Ed. Paul Atkinson et al. Los Angeles: Sage, 2001.

Rushdie, Salman. *Imaginary Homelands: Essays and Criticism, 198–1991*. New York: Penguin, 1981–1991.

Sanmiguel, Inés. *Japan's Quest for El Dorado: Emigration to Colombia*. Tokyo: Kojin-shoten, 2002.

Index

For Product Safety Concerns and Information please contact our EU
representative GPSR@taylorandfrancis.com Taylor & Francis Verlag GmbH,
Kaufingerstraße 24, 80331 München, Germany

Batch number: 08153807

Printed by Printforce, the Netherlands